EARLY HISTORY
OF SINGING

EARLY HISTORY
OF SINGING

BY

W. J. HENDERSON

AMS PRESS
NEW YORK

105 190

Reprinted from the edition of 1921, New York
First AMS EDITION published 1969
Manufactured in the United States of America

Library of Congress Catalogue Card Number: 78-98634

AMS PRESS, INC.
New York, N.Y. 10003

To
Dr. Frank Damrosch
DIRECTOR OF THE INSTITUTE OF MUSICAL ART
NEW YORK CITY

PREFACE

THE aim of this book should be easily deduced from its title. The author has endeavored to trace the development of the modern art of singing from the beginning of the Christian era to the time of Alessandro Scarlatti. He has treated of vocal forms only to the extent requisite to make clear the character of the technic and the style of each period. His main object has been to show what singers were expected to do and as far as possible how they prepared themselves for the delivery of the music placed before them.

The interesting changes brought into vocal art by the advent of opera and later by the action of public taste on the new form of amusement are described and a general survey of early ideals of lyric interpretation and their modifications by the alterations in the demands of audiences is made. Special attention has been given to vocal technic and teaching in the last years of the sixteenth and all of the seventeenth centuries. In treating of this subject in Chapters VIII and IX the author has leaned heavily on the scholarly and admirable work of Hugo Goldschmidt, "Die Italienische Gesangsmethode des XVII Jahrhunderts."

The numerous other authorities consulted in the preparation of this volume are mentioned from time to time in the text. The materials for this work have been accumulated by a slow process of accretion during fifteen years of study of this subject. The author is not acquainted with any other book in which they are thus assembled, and therefore cherishes the hope that this history will prove welcome to singers, teachers of singing, students and music lovers.

CONTENTS

EARLY HISTORY OF SINGING

CHAPTER I

The Dawn of the Art

THE modern art of singing began with the establishment of schools for the study of the correct manner of delivering the liturgical chants of the Roman Catholic church. These chants were derived from still older music used in the ceremonials of Jewish congregations or in the worship of the gods of Egypt and of Greece. Secular song also had a measurable, but comparatively small, influence in the formative period of vocal art, for some of the early fathers found it necessary to warn their followers against the seductions of this style. St. Clement, the second successor of St. Peter, wrote: "It must not be possible to confound us with the singers and buffoons who for a piece of bread or a cup of wine come to divert people who are feasting."

Before the foundation of Christianity the ancients sang in the Temple, in the theatre, and

in the home; but we do not know whether
they possessed anything which we would call
"method." Nor does this greatly signify to us.
Our own art is the child of the Catholic Church
and its history must be traced from the moment
when that church became a single organization,
its functions centralized under the dominion of
one monarch, and its musical style informed by
a well defined purpose.

Until that time this music was uncertain in its
progress, which was distracted by the operation
of numerous agencies, not only musical, but also
religious and political. It is not essential to our
purpose that we should rehearse in detail the
various steps in the march of church music from
the hour when Christ and the apostles sang at
the Last Supper the "Great Hallel" of the Jewish
service. To undertake such a study would involve us in endless difficulties without bringing
sufficiently remunerative results. We should find
ourselves confronted with a mass of fragmentary
information, much of it leading to no conclusions.
Basic facts of vital import would be too often
missing. The most skilful scrutiny of scientific
research has served only to demonstrate that
they are lost beyond recovery. Our best course,
therefore, will be to note some of the most sig-

nificant facts bearing on the earliest history of modern vocal art, and to show briefly how the various influences which gathered about its cradle made their presence felt.

We must, then, recollect that Christianity was born in Judea, where the ceremonials of Moses reigned in the temples devoted to the worship of Jehovah. The country, however, was under the dominion of Rome, and its borders were incessantly crossed by the children of that indomitable empire. At the same time the wily and restless Greeks, both those of the motherland and those of the even more sophisticated blend of Alexandria, were not unknown in the land of Benjamin and Manasseh. Furthermore we must not forget that the excursion of the religion into the world began early. It was at Antioch in Syria a little more than forty years after the birth of the Saviour that his disciples were first called Christians, and it was in this city that a brilliant and powerful branch of the Catholic church speedily grew up. We need hardly be reminded too, that in the middle of the first century St. Paul was writing epistles to churches in Greece itself, and we have what many historians regard as satisfying evidence that St. Peter visited the Christians in Rome.

It will be understood readily that the early influences brought to bear on Christian church music were chiefly Hebrew and Greek, and that out of the materials of these two kinds of song the first chants of the church were made. Of this formative period we can attempt hardly an outline. Its inner history is too obscure and complicated for our edification, even could we be certain that we are in possession of all the facts. We may with profit turn aside for a moment to glance at the moment of solidification of the elements. To do this we must look for an instant at the movement of the Roman world. The story of music has habitually been told as if it had developed without relation to general history or influence by it. But no one can be blind to the tremendous significance of the events which culminated A.D. 324 in the unification of the Roman empire under Constantine. That these events had a bearing on modern music cannot be gainsaid, but in a work such as this they cannot be recounted in detail. We have already intimated that no general system of liturgical chant could exist while the Roman empire, and consequently the Roman church, were divided into so many parts. Nor was the church itself an established institution until Constantine had crushed his great

enemy Maxentius in the west and brought grovel-
ling to his feet Licinius, his sole remaining foe
in the east. The conquest of Byzantium was the
last step toward the reunion of the Roman
dominions, partitioned 37 years earlier by Diocle-
tian. The authoritative establishment of the
Catholic church was not long delayed, though the
cautious Constantine eluded the ceremony of bap-
tism till late in his life.

The music of the early Christians, as we have
already noted, was largely Jewish. The gradual
emancipation of Catholic music from Jewish influences went hand in hand with the swift spread
of Christianity. The parent church of the Christian world was that of Jerusalem, and its first
fifteen bishops were Jews. Its rigid adherence
to Mosaic law and to the ancient ceremonials
of its people aroused frequent, but not quickly
successful, opposition. It was not till the religion
of Jesus had spread into the adjacent lands that
the supremacy of Hebrew law and custom was
overthrown. To the century in which the identity
of the Hebrew body called the Nazarenes was
preserved we owe the characteristics of Jewish
music found in the early Christian chants. To
the rapid spread of Christianity through other
parts of the bulky Roman empire we owe the

introduction of characteristics entirely dissociated from the Hebrew. Those who wish to trace the entire history of this movement of Christianity in its absorbing details should refer to the celebrated fifteenth chapter of Gibbon's "Decline and Fall of the Roman Empire," where the story is told with graphic brilliancy and the philosophy of the events discussed with penetrating insight.

We may now take a swift survey of the early church music with the purpose of determining its nature and the tendencies of its progress. From the very beginning vocal music was engaged in its life-long effort to reach a perfectly artistic equipoise of the two fundamental elements, the literary and the musical. The oldest form of modern art music is the chant and in that form the rhythm, accent and movement of the music are those of the text. This principle followed vocal music into the service of the Christian church, and the early liturgy included portions chanted in a style which possessed melodic sequences of tones, but which had no rhythm, nor measure, and naturally no harmonic basis.

But we shall see that even at the outset, when the fathers of the church had no thought of vocal or musical art, the art principle was present, unrecognized by them. The element of floridity, which passed into the service of the church even as early as St. Paul's time, was the agent of musical freedom. Through it independence of movement eventually found its way into the music of the church, for soon after the singing of several notes to a syllable became permissible the purely musical expressiveness and decorative quality of that style became patent to the fathers. From the time when they found that the beauty of the chant could be heightened in this way we may date all the experiments in real composition.

One feature of the Byzantine chant, adopted from the chants of Syria and Persia, and traced also to the religious song of the Hebrews, becomes significant here. In the intoning of certain texts to fixed chants it was the custom to retain carefully the accented parts of the melodies by joining them to single syllables. When it was impossible to sing the text to the melody without doubling notes the repetitions were always made on the unaccented portions.

Here we discern the elementary form of the syllabic chant, the form which endeavors to give one note—or not more than two—to each syllable. This form may be called the recitative of church music. It is the form in which the simple communications of the liturgy are set forth. In its earliest period, as in its latest, the music of the church reserved its most decorative style for the expression of the higher religious emotions; and in the infancy of the art we find the congregation singing florid phrases in the utterance of the responses which formed essential parts of the antiphonal service.

But the progress of congregational singing did not end here. About the end of the third century it assumed in the church of Persia an importance quite significant. Bardesanes, a leader of the heretic sect of gnostics, brought a new life into the services of his people by composing psalms and hymns in which the congregation had a much larger share than it formerly had when its singing was confined to the responses. The Catholics found it necessary to confront this movement and did so by adopting the new method, which thus spread from Persia into Antioch and thence to the entire Orient.

The plan was to divide the congregation into two demi-choruses, one of men, the other of women and children, each delivering a verse of the psalm. After these two deliveries, one by each choir, both united in singing the refrain. Sometimes this refrain was one of the ancient responses, always brief; sometimes new chants, somewhat longer, were composed. The new style was called "antiphonia," and was introduced into Rome under Pope Damasius, who was pontiff from 366 to 384, into Milan by St. Ambrose in or about 386, and at Constantinople by St. John Chrysostom in 390. This antiphonal singing was certainly as old as the Psalms, and probably was known when Miriam sang her song of triumph. At any rate it belonged to the Jewish church and came thence into these early Christian ceremonials.

We have now before us the two basic elements of modern vocal art, the plain chant and the florid. In the earliest liturgies the latter is found only in the portions allotted to the people, while the syllabic style appears to have been used wholly for the utterances of the priests. In this fact there is a significance which in my opinion has not received sufficient consideration. The singing of responses more or less florid by the congregation, when taken in connection with the texts used for these responses, indicates a tendency, whether conscious or unconscious, to move toward a purely musical expression of emotion.

The early church had two principal liturgies. That of Alexandria and adjoining Egypt was arranged by St. Mark; that of Jerusalem by

St. James, the second bishop of the Judean city. In both of these liturgies the Greek exclamation "Kyrie eleison" appears as a congregational response. We find also (at least in the liturgy of St. James) the Hebrew interjection, "Alleluia," which St. John in his Revelation heard even the celestial choir singing. We find this triumphant praise of the Lord in these eastern liturgies at the close of the Cherubic hymn.

Naturally we have no record of the music which these oriental congregations employed in their alleluias and kyries. But from historical developments of a little later date we were justified in the inference that from the very beginning the restrictions of the rigidly syllabic chant did not apply to the jubilations or the supplications of the people, who were always accorded a wider latitude of musical utterance until the melodic elaborations became too difficult for them. Then the singing of the responses, as well as other parts of the service, was confided to the choir, but the extended manner of treating the syllables handed down from the earliest times was retained. The florid kyrie, amen and alleluia began with the responses of the congregation.

M. Amedée Gastoué, professor of chant in the

Schola Cantorum of Paris, has put forth the
latest and most convincing examination of the
early church music, and his conclusions embrace
the important determination that some chants
have come down to us in the forms known in
Gregory's time. In his "L'Art Grégorien" he
has ably discussed this matter. To set forth
briefly his points, the books of the Roman chant
which have come down to us show a distinct
unity of character. We have not many manu-
scripts, but the fidelity with which they were
reproduced from the second half of the eighth
to the ninth century assures us that we possess
the chants of the Gregorian antiphonary in the
form which they had acquired at that period.
Can we go back further—perhaps to Gregory
himself? Most probably; for beside the unity of
tradition, which is demonstrated, we have a
criterion in the chants themselves.

Internal criticism reveals differences of style
in certain chants. We have the knowledge that
in the second half of the seventh century some
chants were added to the primitive Gregorian
repertory. Hence, when we find chants revealing
a style of a period anterior to these, we are justified in believing that they were preserved in their

authentic form, which the Schola Cantorum guarded and of which that school attributed the editorship to its founder Gregory.

In his masterly articles on the chant in the "Encyclopédie de la Musique et Dictionnaire du Conservatoire" the same author, writing at a later date, defines more clearly his conviction that we have in our possession not only chants of the so-called Gregorian, but even some of the earlier, period, the Ambrosian, preserved with jealous care by the diocese of Milan. He says:

"The character of the Ambrosian melodies, approaching the Gallican and Roman styles, is nevertheless wholly individual. The matter can be summed up briefly thus: in comparison with the Gregorian chant the simple melodies are very simple and the ornate ones very ornate. The simple chants have in general much charm: the luxuriant vocalises, on the other hand, do not present the artistic distinction which the Roman melodies ordinarily show. The study of the Ambrosian repertory is of puissant interest when one compares it with the Roman. In effect the liturgy of Milan has preserved a sufficiently great number of pieces which one finds again in the Gregorian ritual, pieces going back to the formation of these repertoires. The Milanese chant gives

us these pieces in their original state, often de-
faced, while the Roman presents them in an
elaborate artistic form or in the shape of a different variation of the same theme."

The conclusions of M. Gastoué, though not
identical with those of M. Gevaert in his masterly
work on the ancient chant, lie in the same region
in so far as one vital point is concerned, to wit,
that we still possess certain chants in their early
forms and that we therefore have some definite
knowledge of the character and style of Christian
church music of the period of its childhood, at
least as far back as the final years of the fourth
century. For the purposes of the present work
the value of these researches lies in their demonstration of the early entrance of that flexible
vocal style called florid, upon which modern vocal
art reared itself.

The beginnings of this elastic song are to be
found in the Catholic antiphonary. Gastoué invites our attention to his conclusion that the
responses sung by the people in the eastern
churches in the first century were much like those
still used in the daily mass and the minor festivals. He quotes these examples from the Vatican edition of Pope Pius X.

The first of these is in the form of the daily

mass; the others, which are variations of the first, are for minor festivals. These forms were already traditional throughout the Latin church in the tenth century, and M. Gastoué believes that they belonged originally to the antiphonary of Ambrose. At any rate it seems safe to say that they belong to the most ancient relics of Gregorian chant and that they preserve early formulæ employed in congregational responses.

Men had groped after a vocal expression of emotion long before the birth of the Christian church and it is not astonishing that the influence of older manners of praise and jubilation affected the infant song of a new worship. Over two centuries before the Christian era Demetrius Phalerius had noted that the Egyptian priests sang on the vowels in honor of their gods. A little later Nichomachus is telling us that the seven planets produce each a certain sound and that the priests in glorifying their divinity invoked him with inarticulate tones and without consonants. One purpose of this was to propitiate the genii who inhabited the stars of our system. The singing of the proper vowel set in vibration the necessary sympathetic waves.

Engel in his "Music of the Most Ancient Nations" pictures an Assyrian sculpture representing vocal and instrumental musicians welcoming a returning conqueror. "One of the female singers," he notes, "is holding her hand to her throat in the same manner as the women of Syria, Arabia and Persia are in the habit of doing at the present day, when producing on festive occasions those peculiarly shrill sounds of rejoicing which have been repeatedly noticed by Oriental travellers. Dr. Clarke (Travels in Various Countries, E. D. Clark, London, 1810) says, 'They are caused by trilling the tongue against the roof of the mouth without the utterance of any distinct words. Yet this singular mode of expressing joy is all that constitutes the alleluia of the ancients. When Lord Hutchinson first entered Cairo after the capture of the city, he was met by a number of women who greeted him with alleluias; they accompanied him through the streets, clapping their hands and making this extraordinary noise in a loud and shrill tone. It seems to be a constant reiteration of the same syllable uttered with the utmost rapidity.' "

It is unnecessary to our purpose that we should trace the successive steps in the early expansion of the florid element in the musical ritual of the church. We shall see later that florid singing became of large importance and that the ancient practice of carolling on vowels reissued in the form of prolonged cadences on alleluias, amens, kyries and other words, and furthermore that elaborate vocalizations of single vowels, such as the "A" in alleluia or amen, had assumed permanent positions in the service. The attitude of the church toward such song is formulated in some words of St. Augustine written in regard to the "jubili," one of the types of wordless praise. He says:

"He who jubilates does not utter any words, but a joyous sound without words: for it is the spirit lost in joy, expressing it with all its power, but not arriving at a definition of its sense."

We may now make a brief enumeration of the

steps which led to the clearer definition of the modern art of singing.

Early in the fourth century Pope Sylvester founded a school of chant in Rome. In 367 the Council of Laodicea forbade congregational singing and placed the musical service in the hands of the trained choir.

Naturally we know practically nothing about the method of Pope Sylvester's singing school, though we see one of its fruits in the transfer of the service to the choir. But it is safe to conclude that the school was instituted for the study of the chants themselves, and not for that of vocal technic. As we shall see later, the business of committing the chants to memory was one of the most arduous and prolonged tasks of the church singer of these ancient days. But it is as certain as anything can be that, since unity in delivery had to be attained, the schools speedily discovered that they must impart the rudiments of a style. And as soon as this was recognized, the subject of uniform phrasing had to be taken up, and this inevitably led the instructors directly to the consideration of management of the breath. And so from the endeavor to form a style of delivery for the church chant must have come the discovery of the fundamental elements of vocal technic.

Chant is a smooth and flowing kind of melody. Hence its singing requires a perfect legato, and it is beyond question that the rule recently repeated with so much emphasis by the Solesmes fathers, that there must be no approach to staccato in the delivery, was formulated in the earliest days of vocal study. When the instructors in the school of Sylvester had recognized the vital necessity of a pure legato, they must have found themselves confronted with the difficulty of uniting this with a clear enunciation, without which a church service would become a piece of empty sound.

Thus then, the search after a correct style of chant singing carried the early singers directly to the fountains of vocal art. All that remained to be added was a moderate amount of facility in the florid passages, a facility which was destined to develop into unexpected and amazing brilliancy.

CHAPTER II

Vocal Technic of the Early Chanters

Since, when we view them from the distance of the present, the various threads of the early story of singing seem inextricably tangled, a strictly chronological account of the progress of the art is formidably difficult, if not impossible. Furthermore we are not in possession of sufficient information to enable us to trace conclusively the details of progress through the centuries between A.D. 300 and 1600, when the modern opera originated. It seems, then, more practicable to take a rapid view of the condition of vocal technic in the early centuries and afterward to introduce details when they are accessible and applicable to the general story.

Of the state of singing in the formative period of the ecclesiastic chant most students of the history of music have a conception which is largely affected by error. Their conception presents to their minds a chant entirely plain, sung with a broad, sustained legato and with a noble simplicity, alternating with "kyries" and "alleluias" sung in florid music of much elegance and temperate brilliancy.

The truth, however, is that almost in its inception the chant was touched by the luxurious taste of professional singers, and was decorated with those flowers of song which the Italians call "fiorituri." The erroneous belief that modern singing was born somewhere near the close of the sixteenth century has obscured the facts. Singing as an art is probably as old as the Christian era and perhaps much older. At any rate, much of what we regard as belonging to the time of the famous operatic virtuosi came down to us from remote centuries. We may therefore specify three influences which speedily effaced the original simplicity of the chant. These were: (1) The employment of professional singers in the church.

(2) The existence from antiquity of a large stock of vocal technic.

(3) The development, or at least the preservation, of vocal skill by the schools of chant.

Pope Sylvester's school, mentioned in the preceding chapter, is said to have been founded in 314. Its purpose and the inevitable results of its search after a correct style have been set forth.

We may surmise that the chants were sung quite purely for a time, but just how long must remain a matter of conjecture.

Professional singers were known even in ancient Greece. But they differed from the new professionals of the churches in that their art was entirely secular. Plato expressed disapproval of hiring "mercenary musicians" to entertain dinner guests. One of Aristophanes' characters tells how he invited a friend to sing a song of Simonides, and received the answer that singing and playing at dinners had gone out of fashion. Festivals and banquets and theatrical performances were about the only occasions for the services of professional singers. It was against the styles of such singers that the warning of St. Clement, already quoted, was uttered.

The great forward step of the Church was into a practically new art world. When the Council of Laodicea in 367 forbade congregational singing, it placed the musical liturgy in the hands of the canons, or singing men. These alone were permitted to ascend to the ambon, or reading desk, and sing to the congregation. Only clergy could take part in the service, and hence these singers were obliged to take orders of a kind. They were ordained by a presbyter (never by a bishop) with the words prescribed by the fourth council of Carthage: "See that thou believe in thy heart what thou singest with thy mouth, and approve in thy works what thou believest in thy heart." These men were solo chanters, and the appearance of the church soloist is one of the significant events in the history of vocal art. That these solo chanters quickly began to introduce into their singing the ornaments which had existed since a time long before their own is certain. That they speedily acquired the self glory which has clung to singers ever since is proved by the records of contemporaries.

They began to swell with vanity, a product of their position, and soon showed a fondness for certain personal adornment. For one thing they cultivated long hair, "of which the luxuriance, displayed on the soft silken tunics, as the beautiful semi-Byzantine mosaics of St. Come and St. Damien show us, added without doubt, as they thought, to the effect produced by the voice, when in view of all the people they delivered from the ambon the verses of the sacred melody."*

The employment of trained singers in the service of the church in its earliest centuries led

* "L'Art Gregorien," Amadée Gastoué.

to the institution at a later period of the famous Schola Cantorum of Gregory, of which a sketch will be hereinafter given, and this school supplied the singers for the Sistine Chapel, the Papal Choir. Errors of various sorts have crept into the meagre and scattered references to the first years of church singing. Chief of all mistakes have been that which represent the art as without any substantial body of technic and that which depicts the method of delivering the chants as entirely choral, though in unison. The inflated singers above described were soloists and so were some of their successors in the schools of Gregory, as we shall see.

There was a very considerable store of technic ready to be adapted to the uses of the early church. That the chanters developed a style uniting technical finish with elegance is beyond question, and they had accomplished this before the period at which we obtain evidence of the beginnings of part singing, to wit, the end of the ninth century.

In a mass of details, some of which are confusing and others contradictory, one conclusion shapes itself clearly, namely, that the chants were not sung in a dull and monotonous manner. The trained singers filled them with richness and variety. M. Lemaire has well said "the caprice of the artist has always existed." The chanters assumed the right to give freedom to their fancies in the treatment of the melodies and to embellish them just as later singers ornamented madrigals and airs. The passages, vocalises, appoggiaturas and portamenti, of which records have been found in the musical monuments preserved from the early centuries, constitute a body of technic forming the foundation of the entire system of modern florid singing.

The trill, for example, is said to have been known in the first century. It was surely known in the third. Pomponius Festus, the grammarian, who wrote at that time, defines it thus: "Vibrissare est vocem in cantando crispare." The term which he here explains is "vibrissare," a technical term of singing, and "crispare" means to shake backward and forward, to brandish.

The portamento undoubtedly entered into the delivery of the chant very early, for singers whose training was so largely devoted to the formation of a standard style must soon have discovered the adaptability of the liquid consonants to the creation of a vocal effect. But we find no written record of the matter till that

of Guido of Arezzo, who flourished in the first
half of the eleventh century. He said:

"Liquescunt in multis voces, more litterarum,
ita ut inceptus modus unius ad alterum limpide
transiens nec finiri videatur."

(The voices melt together in many after the
manner of the letters, so that one tone begun
seems limpidly flowing into another and not to
be completed.)

It is true that Emilius Probus, a grammarian
of the fourth century, had used the verb "liques-
cere" to describe the melting together of m,l,n
and r with other consonants, but this passage
from Guido is the first account we have of the
musical effect. Undoubtedly this portamento was
not far away when Probus wrote. In their "Gregorian Music" the Benedictines of Stanbrook
describe the effect as used in our own time:

"As in the alphabet there are liquids so there
are liquid sounds. These occur at the passage
from one syllable to another when a note which
began full and entire expires. as it were, and
is fused with the next note."

Diminutions or divisions existed in an elementary form from the very beginning of florid
chant, as shown in the previous chapter. It re-

mained for them to acquire that special treatment which entered with the art of "descant."
In the eleventh century we find the first use of
these vocal variations. The singer's method was
to take the prescribed notes of the chant and
divide them into shorter ones.

This species of embryonic counterpoint was
improvised in the beginning; and, rapidly becoming extremely ornate, it not only gave great latitude to the singer, but demanded of him skill,
taste and sound musicianship. Its use obliged
singers to make serious studies and to exercise
their imaginations. The exacting courses of the
schools made almost every singer a composer,
and the facility in invention acquired through
constant practice prevented their vocal virtuosity
from becoming cold and dull.

Marks of expression were known at least as far back as the closing years of the eighth century. That the graces of expression itself were employed earlier cannot be doubted in view of the history of these marks. When Charlemagne was in Rome for the Easter festivals of 787, he was so impressed by the superiority of the Roman chanters that he begged Pope Adrian to assign to him two cantors of the Gregorian school and to furnish each of them with an authentic copy of the antiphonary. The chosen men were Peter and Romanus, who set out for Germany in 789. At the monastery of St. Gall Romanus fell sick and remained behind. Peter went to Metz and founded a famous school. The monks of St. Gall begged Charlemagne to leave Romanus with them. He finished his life there, established a school of Gregorian chant, and left his antiphonary to the abbey. In training the heavy and rebellious voices of the Germans he introduced the marks of expression called after him, "romanian letters."

The letters were written in small text above the neumes, the notation of the period. It is unnecessary to go into all the details of the subject. The most important were those which affected tempo or rhythm. These were C, standing for "celeriter," which called for an accelerando; T, meaning tenere (to hold); M, mediocriter, or moderato. There were also letters denoting degrees of force and others indicating modifying words, such as "bene," or "mediocriter." For instance b is frequently used to modify T, thus giving an equivalent to our *molto ritardando*.

The study of the voice itself undoubtedly began early, for before 1300 the division of the scale into registers was known. At what time attention was first directed to this much discussed matter cannot be determined. But from various hints we may reasonably conclude that the teachers, while recognizing the registers, made no attempts at equalizing the scale, except such as would occur naturally in the search after smoothness and beauty. Marchetto, a writer of about 1300, tells us that one of the ornaments of singing in his day was to pass from the chest to the falsetto—after the manner of a jodel. The student of the subject may find something to ponder in the words of Jerome of Moravia (13th century): "Different kinds of voices ought not to be mingled in the chant, whether it be chest with head or throat with head. . . . Generally low voices and basses are of the chest, light and high voices of the head, and those of the throat intermediate. They should not be mixed in chant, but chest voice should remain such just as the voice of the throat or the head."

Falsetto voices were common at least as far back as this period and were condemned by severe disciplinarians. Basses, on the other hand, were regarded as objectionable when they were of the loudest kind. They were aptly called "voces taurinae." Whether castrati were employed in the earliest centuries is doubtful. At least there is no trustworthy information on the subject. On the other hand the familiar assertion that they were first known after the period of the Spanish falsettists is equally questionable, seeing that it is almost certain that there were eunuchs with soprano voices in the choruses of ancient Assyria. There is furthermore a tradition that the eastern chant was introduced into Smolensk, Russia, by Manuel, a castrato. This must have been about the beginning of the eleventh century. However these disassociated incidents have no important bearing on the history of modern singing. The salient facts in regard to the early knowledge of voice registers and their uses, possessed by the

Italians, have now been given and they serve to show that the art had made no inconsiderable progress before the twelfth century.

The most potent agency in forwarding the development of singing in the middle ages was the Schola Cantorum of Rome, founded by Gregory the Great, and it now becomes essential that we examine the influences which produced this school and then the methods of the school itself.

CHAPTER III

The Schola Cantorum

THE western empire of Rome reached its in-
glorious end when Odoacer dethroned Romulus
Augustus and proclaimed himself King of Italy
in A.D. 476. From this date we reckon the period
called the middle ages, which terminated with
the fall of Constantinople in 1453. The over-
throw of Rome completed the ruin of her schools,
which had been gradually disintegrating during
the continued attacks of the barbarians.

Marcus Aurelius Cassiodorus, a Roman of
senatorial rank, father of Boethius, the celebrated
writer on music, flourished in the middle years
of the sixth century, and about 535 undertook
the reorganization of the schools. He raised
funds by subscripion and himself wrote the
manual of instruction to be used by the teachers.
The fifth chapter of this work treated of music
and was the basis of the musical study of the
time. The treatise is lost, but there can be no
doubt that Gregory was acquainted with its doc-

trines. Cassiodorus took holy orders and founded a monastery. Gregory was a student there and became the first abbot. The musical method in use was that of Benoit (died about 540) and in this were brought together the usages which came to have the force of law throughout the western church. This method, or practice, set forth numerous details as to the execution of the chant.

Now the abbot had general surveillance of the office, and also had charge of the singing boys. Gregory became a deacon, which means that he was one of the choir singers; and soon after he became Pope in 590 he founded the Schola Cantorum, the school of singers which established the authoritative delivery of the musical liturgy for all Europe.

From the various schools directed by the church pupils with good voices were selected for training in the Schola Cantorum. They became inmates of the dormitories of the Pontifical establishment and pensionaires, except in the cases of children of noble birth, who received no pensions. All were educated in the several liberal arts. They were under the immediate direction of the masters of chant, called paraphonists. These were four in number, named, in order of rank, primicier, secundicier, and so forward. In

due course the title of paraphonist was conferred
on the most skilful of the pupils, such as were
competent to sing the solos of the "alleluia."

The period devoted to the studies of the Schola
Cantorum was nine years. The instruction was
both theoretical and practical, but the length of
the time of study was demanded chiefly by the
requirement that all the chants should be memor-
ized. Only the director or the soloist was permitted to have a book. In the classes the teacher
was seated at the monochord, from which the
pitch was communicated to the students.

All the singers, boys as well as men, had their
heads shaved and wore chasubles. In the proces-
sion the singers marched in two ranks, the instructors outside, the boys inside, and in the
chancel they retained this order. The choirs
were small. They were generally in groups of
about twenty or thirty soloists. The ensembles of
the service were sung by the choir, the clergy and
the congregation, but the most important parts
were reserved for the trained vocalists. It is not
difficult to present to the imagination the character of the singing of these artists, selected with
scrupulous care and rigorously trained. The
voices must have possessed the power and flexibility which we have long associated with the best

Italian singing.   Something of the ancient style is preserved in the present choral body of the Sistine Chapel and certain other churches in Rome.   The visit of the so-called Vatican Choirs to the United States in the autumn of 1919 gave many music lovers opportunity to hear the masterpieces of the later church composers sung by a choir of this kind, but of pure Gregorian music nothing was offered.

The supreme test of vocal progress in the epoch making school was ability to sing solo music of a type elegantly, if not what we should now regard as brilliantly, florid.   Upon the history of the diffusion of the teachings of the Schola Cantorum we need not linger.   The story would prove neither entertaining nor instructive.   But we may pause to make note of the significant development of luxuriance of style in the eastern church, where the chant had already risen to sufficient importance to command the attention of Justinian.

We must also take account of the ancient Spanish chant, called Mozarabic or Visigothic, which was submerged by the Roman chant before the eleventh century.   But floridity was a feature of the Spanish church music, certainly a bequest of the Moors, if not of the Visigoths, whom they

succeeded. The artistic circle was completed by
the reaction of Oriental influences on Spanish
music. Leander, archbishop of Seville, author of
many pieces of church music all richly vocalized,
passed some years in Constantinople during the
period of the highest development of the chant
of the eastern church. He became acquainted
with Gregory, who at that time was "apocrisiary"
(or papal representative) at the eastern court.
Unfortunately few actual records of the Mozara-
bian chant have survived, but the opulence of its
floridity has been thoroughly established by the
researches of Pierre Aubry, and its direct influence on certain compositions in the field of
Roman chant demonstrated.

From the confused mass of fragmentary information that has come down to us we need
select only two important facts. All the music
of the early eastern church was elegantly florid.
In general these chants were for solo singers;
the choir sang only the refrain, the alleluia, and
the final doxology (Gloria in excelsis). The
melodies, very free in rhythm, were quite free
in movement, like recitative. They were sometimes simple and at others decorated with long
vocalises. For instance the "prokeimenon," a
responsory part of the liturgy, was sung to a

chant vocalised at length and introducing trills. The famous "Parthenion" of St. Methodius, archbishop of Tyre (died 312) consists of a series of strophes written after the manner of the psalms. There is a solo and the chorus repeats continually the same refrain.

The history of the florid ecclesiastic music is well told in other works and need not be rehearsed at further length here. Students of musical history are familiar with the story of the foundation of the famous school at St. Gall. The growth of the sequences also belongs to the general history of the art. The principle underlying the music of the middle ages remained fixed until the advent of the art of descant, which we shall presently consider. This principle, as exemplified in the practice of musicians and singers, demanded, or at least invited, a free application of decoration to the chant and, at least in certain periods, to the portions which would most readily suggest such treatment even to the modern mind. Of the character of these chants we may get some idea from brief excerpts. Here is an example in two successive forms, first the Ambrosian (early fourth century) and second the Roman or Gregorian (sixth century) quoted from Prof. Gastoué's article on primitive chant in the "Encyclopedie de la Musique," published by the Paris Conservatoire:

A traditional "kyrie" of the St. Gall type is found in the codex of the institution. It reads as follows:

A' more elaborately developed type of floridity is found in a composition of Berno, Abbot of Reichenau, a St. Gall pupil who died in 1048.

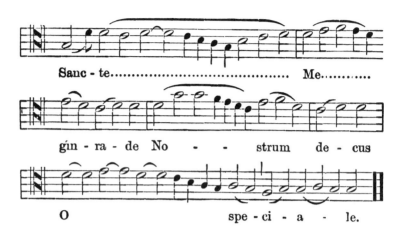

Sanc - te... Me............

gin - ra - de No - - strum de - cus

O   spe - ci - a - le.

These should be sufficient to satisfy the reader
that the general character of the music of the
Christian church from its beginnings in the lands
to the eastward of the Mediterranean was ornate.
The syllabic chant survived because it was suited
to the requirements of the utterance of the priest
and we possess it to-day in the form of the intoned service. But the musical portions of the
liturgy leaned always to a style flexible and elegant, a style which appropriately harmonized with
the architectural surroundings of the devotional
exercises.

In the music itself we have proof that the art
of singing must have reached a level of cultivation far beyond that ascribed to it before the
researches of recent scholars had unearthed so

many splendid relics of the middle ages. We have already taken a swift view of the field of vocal technic and it will presently be necessary to consider what effect the introduction of the art of descant had on vocal practice. But before doing so we should note that the chant maintained its dominance in ecclesiastic music till the eleventh century. It then began a slow retreat before the advancing movement of polyphonic composition, and finally receded to a position analogous to that of seventeenth century opera recitative which served to introduce the arias.

Throughout this period the character of the chant remained unchanged except in exterior features of style. Assuredly, musical antiquarians can determine with confidence an Ambrosian from a Gregorian chant and can with no difficulty point out well-defined traits of the later manners of the schools of Italy and France. But in examining old music with a view to arriving at a knowledge of the state of singing in the centuries between the infancy of Christianity and the advent of the polyphonic masterpieces of church music we need not concern ourselves with peculiarities of local or sectional chants. All that we require is the information, unavoidably drawn from the music itself, that the technic of singing to which the search after uniform style directed the first studies of Pope Julian's fourth century schools, assumed a firmly outlined shape in the Schola Cantorum. The familiar stories of the missions of the Gregorian teachers to Metz and even to Britain have revealed to us the methods by which the singing of the chant was improved through Europe. It is not essential to our purpose to repeat these stories.

What we learn from the monuments of these early centuries is that singing demanded first of all a command of long flowing phrases, the fundamental requisite of a vocal art similar to that demanded by the classic operas of the Handelian era. It is evident that a perfect legato was the base of all singing for not less than eighteen centuries, and that violent attack, forcing of tone, and the clarion delivery of high notes came to be popularly desired in the early part of the nineteenth century.

Upon the basis of this elegant and fluent legato was reared the undulating floridity of the chant. This floridity possessed none of the characteristics found in the amazing cadenzas of the eighteenth century singers. It was not brilliant or sparkling as later music was, but smooth, graceful, aristocratic in character, and frequently

decorated with portamento effects, as described
in the previous chapter.

The pupils of the Schola Cantorum, possessing
all the finesse of its art, naturally sought to enrich
the sacred chant with ornaments which must have
seemed marvellous to their contemporaries. Plain
chant dominated all music up to the thirteenth
century and there existed in the text certain words
on which the singers were at liberty to give reign
to their fancies. Reference already has been
made to the "jubili." The vowels on which these
were sung were called "evovae," a title which
instantly recalls the Greek "evoe." Later the
word "alleluia" filled the same office. St. Udalric
writes "The alleluia is chanted at the end of a
sequence with a neume or a jubilus and the
letter *A* is repeated through numerous modulations." These embroideries were sometimes
longer than the chant itself and many authors
complain of the prominence accorded to "this
kind of vocal fantasia."

Of the manner of singing them we obtain testimony from Walter Odington's "De Speculatione
Musicae" (about 1350) in which he says that the
ornaments of the chant should be executed in a
light voice and without words. Long, florid passages were sung on the "Kyrie," the "Amen,"

"In saecula saeculorum" and similar texts. The manuscript of the celebrated mystery play, "The Wise and Foolish Virgins," which dates from the tenth century, is rich in ornamentation.

This state of sacred music continued till the fourteenth century. Secular music now advanced to a defined place in art and the pope and subaltern church authorities perceived that ecclesiastic music could retain its distinction only by the abolition of its luxurious decorations. A vigorous effort was made to restore the absolutely plain chant. At the beginning of the fourteenth century Pope John XXII ordered the discontinuance of all ornaments. His famous bull, "docta sanctorum," was issued in 1323 and applied not only to ornamentation but to the use of mensural music. W. S. Rockstro, the distinguished English historian of the art, is doubtful whether the order of John endured long, because his successor Benedict XII (1334-42) was very fond of elaborate ceremonials. The Papal court was now at Avignon and the school in Rome followed its ancient traditions, while at the new seat of the Holy See French and Flemish singers, already celebrated, were cordially welcomed.

An important side light is thrown on the state of singing in these centuries by the words of

St. Bernard (1090-1153) in his regulations of
the chant at Citeaux: "It is necessary that men
sing in a virile manner and not with voices shrill
and artificial like the voices of women, or in a
manner lascivious and nimble like actors." He
added cautions that singers should "manage their
respiration" and not sing through the nose.

The words of St. Bernard indicate pretty
clearly that the male soprano was already employed in the church choir. When his entry into
the body was effected must remain doubtful, but
it is reasonable to deduce from the passage quoted
that these singers were not castrati but falsettists.
Indeed historical research has, as already intimated, led toward the conclusion that in western
Europe the falsettists antedated the others. We
shall recur to this topic in a later chapter.

To return to the floridity of the chant, it appears from the "Salmi Passaggiati" (1615) of
Francesco Severi that in the sixteenth century
ornaments on the chants sung in the Sistine
Chapel were continually used. Without enter-
ing too minutely into the details of such information as we find scattered through various
old works, let us endeavor to summarize the
floridity of the chant from the time of Charlemagne to the close of the sixteenth century.

Baini (1775-1844), the distinguished biographer of Palestrina, learned from manuscript letters at Rheims, Metz and Soissons, written to Pepin and Charlemagne by some of the Popes, the meaning of some of the romanian letters and the terms which they represented. Several theoreticians of later date left explanations of the technical terms applied to features of the chant and in the final analysis we learn that all of them relate to ornamentation.

In brief these are the terms: crispatio, trepidatio, reverberatio, vinnulae, voces tremulae, copula, hocheti. "Crispatio" may be translated readily by reference to the definition of Festus already given. It was one of the terms signifying trill. "Trepidatio" was another term meaning a tremble or shake. "Reverberatio" is medieval Latin, not classic, and probably means what later came to be known as beats, the beginning of our vibrato. "Vinnulae" means sweet and its application to vocal technic can only be conjectured. It seems not extravagant to infer that it referred to the use of a soft mezza voce. "Voces tremulae" cannot well be misunderstood. The execution of this grace required breath control of a high order, since it was usually employed in the prolonged final cadences. It is worth mentioning here that the name "trillo" does not appear till the "Nuove Musiche" of Caccini, early in the seventeenth century, while Tosi writing in 1723 declares that this ornament has been entirely abandoned.

The "copula" belongs to the period of part singing, since it means a passage sung by the tenor over a hold by the bass. Jean de Garlandia, writing in the eleventh century, held it to be so desirable that without it perfection in song was impossible. The term "hochetus" meant the detached note or staccato, but in describing compositions it was applied to passages in syncopation. Appoggiaturas, both double and single, ascending and descending, were known in the eleventh century. Of the portamento we have already spoken, while the use of numerous grupetti must be obvious to the reader.

If we possessed histories of the singers of these centuries and descriptions of their styles we should have a tolerably satisfactory view of the condition of musical art from the dawn of Christianity to the advent of the polyphonic school of composition. But only a few names have come down to us. Gregory the Great was undoubtedly a chanter of supreme skill. He was an abbot, a deacon and an archdeacon in turn, and each of these offices carried with it musical duties. An abbot had charge of the school of his abbey, while deacons were the singers of the ornate parts of the liturgy, and were therefore vocal virtuosi. Many epitaphs of such deacons exist and inform us that they were celebrated for their voices and skill. Among others Leon, Redemptus and Sabinus are named. Of the latter his chanting is described as "sweet as nectar and honey." We read of "placid modulations," of psalms chanted on "melodies rich and with varied sounds." James, first master of chant in the churches of Northumberland, England, about 670, is mentioned, as well as Theodore and Benoit, the two famous singers sent by Pope Adrian I into France at the request of Charlemagne. Several popes were graduates of the Schola Cantorum and among those who gained renown as chanters were Sergius I, Gregory II, Etienne II, Paul I, Leo III and Sergius II.

After the Roman school had reached its zenith and wars terminated its development the further advance of the art was made in France, where musicians soon devised a larger and more elastic style than that of the Italians. Doubtless the same artistic spirit which conceived the French Gothic architecture was the inspiration of the splendid style of ecclesiastic music which glorified the liturgy of the new temples. But this topic lies beyond the confines of our subject.

The next step in this study of early singing must be toward an examination of the introduction of mensural music and polyphonic composition, and the character of the vocal art employed in their delivery. Again we must swiftly survey a large field and ask the reader to accept the general facts of musical history as already established.

CHAPTER IV

THE TROUBADOURS, DESCANT AND MENSURAL MUSIC

THE influences which combined to affect the development of song in the eleventh and twelfth centuries were so numerous and closely intertwined that the task of unravelling the threads of the web is well nigh impossible. They may be classified as follows:

The music of the troubadours.

Polyphonic composition.

The art of descant (also called "discant").

Mensural music.

The period of troubadour art extended from at least the middle of the twelfth century to the closing years of the thirteenth. Polyphonic composition may be said to date from the first crude experiments in harmony, of which our earliest records come down from about A.D. 900. The art of discant, as distinguished by the practice of singers from the written polyphony of composers, must have originated almost as soon as part writing, for Hucbald, the Benedictine monk of St. Armand in Flanders, our authority on the beginnings of harmony, mentions a kind of florid improvisation by singers to which the title "descant" was applied in the eleventh century by de Salomon and the Latin appellation *contrapunctus a mente* by Marchetto and Johannes de Muris in the fourteenth century.

The period of mensural music cannot be determined, since it must have existed at least in dance forms from very ancient times; but that of its notation, which covers the time of our written records of it, is set by Johannes Wolf in the title of his important work, "Geschichte der Mensural Notation von 1250-1460."

It is unnecessary to linger on the musicianship of the troubadours. The long accepted belief that these knightly singers were poets and not composers has been proved fallacious by the labors of Pierre Aubry and Jean Beck. We know now that most of the troubadours were trained musicians, educated in abbeys and receiving the courses of instruction followed by young men preparing to take holy orders. These courses inevitably included ecclesiastic song, and the creations of the troubadours show clearly that their art was the child of a marriage of sacred and profane music with the language of the people as the uniting agent.

Ancient secular songs going back at least as far as the ninth century (see Coussemaker), "Histoire de la Harmonie au Moyen Age") show us that the spirit of music moved among the people with its customary contempt for the teachings of the schools. But somewhat later, at the point whence we can trace the most ancient of the lays of the troubadours, we discover that the influence of ecclesiastic composition was not unfelt in secular music.

Side by side with these lays we meet secular songs of which the music was palpably a mere replica of the ecclesiastical, as in the cases of the "complaints" and certain settings of odes of Horace. The "lai," which is probably the oldest surviving form of the ancient Celtic art, was unquestionably popular in character. Among these lays, written to verses of irregular lengths, we find ornamentations of cadenza-like nature, indubitably suggested by the florid terminations of psalms or the elegant exfoliations of the St. Gall sequences. On the other hand, we more frequently meet with simpler forms of floridity, clearly used for both expressive and decorative purposes. Here is an example of the most elaborate St. Gall style, the termination of an "Alleluia" by Notker Balbulus, the father of the St. Gall school:

Alleluia, Notker Balbulus.

Al - le - lu - jah.

Turning to one of the earliest relics of troubadour song, we may note the simpler floridity already mentioned:

Quant li lou - sei - gnolz jo - lis chante

sur la flor - d'e - sté que naist la ro - se

et   le lys et la   ro - sée et–vert pre.

This old song antedates the works of the
masters restudied and adequately revealed by
Johannes Wolf. As a piece of troubadour composition it exemplifies the kind of music written
by a nobleman educated in an abbey and composing under the influence of church music, but
to secular text with clearly definite rhythm. In
it we see some of the earliest specimens of an
employment of floridity, which became conventionalized. The expansion of the melody in a
decorative design on the words "flor" and "rosee"
belongs distinctly to the type of vocal art which
utilizes floridity to combine external imitation
with fanciful suggestion. It is a direct endeavor
to employ a grace of music to convey a thought.
It is primitive tone painting.

Let us not suppose that this kind of floridity

began with the Chatelaine de Coucy (whose music has been quoted), or even with the troubadour body of songsters; but from their day its development in modern vocal composition can be clearly traced, and mayhap some historian, who has yet before him the years needed for the task, will be tempted to follow in its details the march of floridity from this estate of naïve beauty and delineation to its highest elevation and thence downward to its subsequent banality.

Naturally we next turn our eyes to the elegant floridity of the *Ars Nova.** Beauty derived from the exercise of artistic purpose in music is perhaps not so young as historians have asked us to believe. It is incontestable that in the creation of the massive forms of church counterpoint the assembling of the technical materials occupied all the laborers till Josquin de Pres came to his maturity and found the clay ready for his moulding. The first works of imposing beauty in the field of church counterpoint were his; but beauty in simpler vocal music had existed for at least two centuries before his time, and the composers of the *Ars Nova* period show a keen and almost unerring instinct for the employment of the graces

*A title applied to the early works written in mensural notation, whether by troubadours or others.

and decorative features of song both as elements of pure musical beauty and as means of suggestion or expression.

They preserved the traditions of secular floridity in their musical settings of such words as "fior," "amore," "paradiso," and all the others which had come to be conventionally associated with thrills of ecstasy to be expressed in a gorgeous exfoliation of the melody. One finds that the verb "cantare" invariably suggests the introduction of a display of vocal technic. Indeed, the most extraordinary feats of the composers and vocal virtuosi of the baroque opera (late 17th century) or of the post-Handelian decadence could not outdo the achievements of the *Ars Nova*. The vowel sound "ah" is already established as the favorable medium of display. Here is a characteristic example from a two-voiced song by Lorenzo, of Florence, a fourteenth century writer. The text is taken from Wolf.

On the other hand there are many passages which prove that these early writers had already begun to disregard textual considerations. They respected conventions and continued them; but where no tradition governed, they wrote florid passages on such words as "per," "un" and even "e."

Pro- ser - pi - na can - ta - - -

As already noted, the vowel sound "ah," which was so favorable to the Italian's emission of tone, was almost invariably vocalized at great length. Arteaga, writing in the latter half of the eighteenth century, was astonished because Pasquale Anfossi (1736-1797) in his "Antigone" employed nine measures of 16 notes each, or 144 notes in all, on the second vowel of the word "amato." Yet we have seen Lorenzo four centuries earlier writing eleven and one-half measures in ancient time of three whole notes to the bar on the second vowel of "cantava."

It should be noted at this point that these extended passages were not as long in duration of time as they look to us on paper. The notation of the early period was practised on a large scale. The whole note signifies a. much longer tone now than it did in the days when composers set up a time signature of 3. It would probably be correct for us to regard the 3 of Lorenzo as equivalent to our three-fourth or possibly three-eighth measure.* But while this gives a just view of the breath support demanded of these ancient singers, it does not in any way modify our deductions as to the attitude of the composers toward the nature and purpose of the florid passage.

The pages of the composers of the great epoch

* For a masterly examination of this matter see "The Interpretation of the Music of the XVIIth and XVIIIth Centuries," by Arnold Dolmetsch. London, 1915.

of polyphonic church music, masters who wrote also secular songs, show no definite aim at florid setting of words or vowels. I have read many hundreds of pages of their scores in the vain effort to discern any organized system in the employment of floridity except that dictated by the immediate demands of the canonic subject. The fluent passages are all essential parts of the musical thought, and their creation seems to be wholly the result of a feeling for the architectural interdependence of the voice parts. In other words, these masters were engaged in making beautiful musical designs with religious expression as the ultimate attainment. In the art of these writers one finds that combination of decoration with general expression that is to be observed in the church architecture of their time. The expression is not reached by means of delineative details, but by the sum total of effects, most of which are essentially decorative in themselves.

The musicians of the formative years of polyphonic writing conceived vocal melody as a smooth flowing river of polished cantilena, unruffled except by an elegant floridity, as well in keeping with its character as sun touched wavelets with the surface of a stream. The troubadours preserved toward song the same attitude as the church writers, but their employment of the language of their people instead of Latin (used in the church texts) compelled them to write in rhythmic manner and not in the prose style of the chant. The results of this step are disclosed in the subsequent history of composition rather than that of singing, and hence do not properly fall within the province of this work.

Polyphonic composition in the broad sense means any kind of part writing, from the simplest two-part harmony to the complex creations of Tallis or Byrd. With its development from the crude "organum" of Hucbald to the works of Palestrina we have no concern. Attention, however, has already been called to the early drawn distinction between *contrapunctus a penna* and *a mente,* and in the latter, the work of the singers, we are directly interested.

Franco, a distinguished theoretician (11th and 12th centuries), has left us a definition of descant as "the simultaneous and harmonious sounding of two or more diverse melodies, which are made equal to one another proportionately by the use of sounds of three degrees of length, represented in writing by the figures of the long, breve, and semibreve." In the explanation of details he informs us further that among the several varieties of descant were that with the same words in all the parts, that with different words, and still another with words in one part and none in others. In order to understand what might be the musical outcome of such varying methods we must bear in mind that the authorities made a clear distinction between descant which was written in mensural music, and "organum purum," in which the plain song tenor was "ultra mensuram" (outside of measure).

The term "tenor" in connection with the old ecclesiastical music means the voice which sang the cantus firmus, or chant melody, and around which other parts grouped themselves; and since in the early stage of the art this cantus firmus was customarily entrusted to the highest male voice, the word "tenor" slowly acquired its modern meaning. Originally it was regarded simply as a derivative of "teneo" ("I hold") and referred to the fact that this voice, to use a modern colloquialism, "carried the tune."

However, at the time when part singing became prevalent (15th century) women certainly enjoyed the privilege of joining with men in the delivery of frottole and strambotti. Bartolomeo Tromboncino's frottola "Signora, anzi mea dea," Nicolo Pifaro's "Piangete occhi dolenti," and many others give the melody to the soprano voice. Unless we are willing to believe that boys or male sopranos were to be found in every chorus and household, we must conclude that women sang in the polyphonic works of the time. We shall discuss this matter further.

About the general rules of descant information besides that of Franco comes from several old writers, and is well summarized in the writings of Johannes Tinctoris (14th century). He tells us that written counterpoint is ordinarily called "res facta." The title "counterpoint" was more exactly applied to improvisation. Without following him into technicalities we learn that the principal law of descant was that the voices should meet always on the consonances, and there seemed to be little concern about the notes between these. He specifically declares that when two, three, four, or more improvise on a chant, no one is subject to the other. "It suffices if each of the singers accords with the tenor in what concerns the movement and order of the concords." Somewhat naïvely to our minds, he adds that he does not blame, but rather praises those singers who give their first consideration to the placing of the concords, because thus they produce a more agreeable and smooth harmony.

Cerone in "Il Melopeo" (Naples, 1613) is the last author who writes about the *contrapunctus a mente*. He tells that it was of two kinds; in one species every one varied his part, and immense skill was needed to prevent confusion. In the other kind one singer alone decorated his part with such ornaments as his imagination suggested, while the others sang the music as it was written.

descant [handwritten margin note]

When singing the first variety, the rule was that the chanters of the different parts should take turns in embroidering; but Cerone tells us that the rule was often broken and some singers made it a point of honor to vocalize in ensemble. He says "Instead of producing a graceful and elegant effect, they succeeded only in giving an imitation of the Jews wailing in their synagogue or a festive reunion of peasants."

Cerone left us 156 pages of examples of the kind of vocal ornamentations used in his day.

The art of *contrapunctus a mente*, then, connects the medieval flowers of song directly with modern operatic art, for the method used by the descanter was in effect that employed by the first prima donna. The ancient descanter embroidered the cantus firmus by dividing its notes into shorter ones and singing his passage in the

diminution [handwritten margin note]

same time as the tenor occupied in singing the cantus firmus. This division of long notes into figures formed of shorter ones came to be called "diminution," and the "running" of diminutions was one of the feats of the earliest public singers of the lyric stage. Furthermore this method of varying a melody became common in instrumental music, and all music lovers are acquainted with one of its most beautiful examples, that of Beethoven's fifth symphony, in which the melody of the slow movement is repeated to us twice in increasing diminutions.

Naturally this kind of "counterpoint," improvised and ornamented, afforded much liberty to the singer and in the end compelled him to give serious attention to his musicianship. The persistence of improvisation, despite the growth of written counterpoint, is instructive because it invites us to believe the medieval music lover to be quite as easily mastered by vocal virtuosity as his successors of the modern opera house. Fortunately for the art the most distinguished singers were theoreticians or composers and were competent to improvise artistically. Among the most famous may be mentioned Franco and Perotin, who lived in the last years of the 11th and first of the 12th century, Philip de Vitry, Jerome of Moravia, Marchetto of Padua, Johannes de Muris and Walter Odington, the Briton, all of the 13th century, Simon Dunstede, Glareanus and Franchinus Gaffori, of the 14th and part of the 15th.

That all was not ideal in the realm of descant we learn from a stern rebuke administered to incompetent singers by Johannes de Muris. He says: "How can men have the face to sing descant who know nothing of the combination of sounds! Their voices roam around the cantus firmus without regard to any rule. They cannot tell a consonance from a dissonance."

This brief comment deepens our conviction that the art of descanting was one imperatively demanding musicianship on the part of the singer. Another impatient exclamation from the far off past satisfies us that the vocal virtuoso of the time, who differed so greatly from his modern successor in the matter of scholarship, at least resembled him in certain visible accompaniments of his art. The Scotch abbot Oelred, writing in the 12th century, tells us that the singers whinny like horses, use gestures, sway their bodies, twist their lips, roll their eyes and even bend their fingers with each note.

CHAPTER V

VOCAL TEACHERS AND SECULAR SONG

THE survey of the state of vocal art in the period of the descanters should suffice to convince us that the path to the brilliant period of the late fifteenth century, when the Italian opera swam into the ken of southern Europe, was thoroughly cleared. But if we turn our attention to the birth of opera, we find ourselves confronted with a considerable army of secular singers equipped with a brilliant technic. Whence came these artists? Whence came their art? It is now our duty to seek the answers to these questions.

The subject has been dismissed curtly in musical histories. We have been funished with generous information concerning composers and their works and their influence upon succeeding schools. But who were the masters of voice? Whom did they teach and what? Let the last inquiry have precedence. The ground has been cleared in the previous chapters. They taught the kind of music that we have considered, and we need henceforth refer to it only as it becomes an inseparable part of the story.

The musical art of the golden age of church counterpoint was vocal. The masterpieces of Josquin des Pres, Hobrecht, Brumel, Lasso, and Palestrina were polyphonic *a cappella* works. Instrumental composition was in its infancy at the moment when the unaccompanied vocal works were crossing their zenith. In the development of the system of polyphonic composition the practice of the singer's descant slowly retired from its prominence. It inevitably gave way to the written text, for only in recorded form could the splendid masses of the Netherlands masters and their disciples be offered for habitual repetition in the services of the church. The improvisation of the singer ultimately confined itself to the decoration of the written text. It assumed a position similar to that of the later ornamentation by the opera singer. But this decoration was created by vocalists who were already thoroughly schooled musicians, and these singers were also the teachers of the art which they practised.

In the earlier stages of the progress of vocal art singing was taught only to those destined to officiate in the services of the church. But

it is probable that from the time of the troubadours singing as an art attracted the attention
and invited the study of some laymen. Consideration of this aspect of the matter may be
postponed for the time in order that we may
first survey the work of the teachers.

It seems to have escaped the notice of many
historians that nearly every one of the great
masters of church counterpoint was a singer and
a teacher of singing. It is unnecessary to go
further back than the time of Guido of Arezzo,
who died in 1050. The histories record fully
the nature of his labors in notation and in the
invention of the system of solmization; but despite
the fact that they tell us that he devised this
system to aid in the instruction of his pupils, they
neglect to emphasize the other fact that he was
one of a long line of teachers of singing. He
was engaged in singing and in training singers
for the glory of the church. It seems likely that
his labor tended rather toward improvements in
intonation than toward voice production, but in
his "Micrology" there is a chapter on the puri-
fication of style and this inclines us to the belief
that he was also what we might call a coach in
interpretation or manner. But without doubt his
pupils, although they included no less a personage

than Pope John XIX, were professional singers of church music. By some of them the methods of Guido were handed down to a still later generation.

If we keep before our minds the fundamental fact that the famous masters of the period extending from the 13th to the 15th centuries were not players upon instruments, but singers and composers of music to be sung, we shall grasp the essential facts of the story. Not till the great organists began to appear did composers of music other than vocal assume importance in the development of the tonal art.

Turning then to the golden age of church counterpoint, we find that Johannes Okeghem, who is generally regarded as the father of the Netherlands school, had attained the position of first singer of the chapel of Charles VII at an early age. He was the teacher of the celebrated Josquin des Pres; but this master already, while still a member of the choir of the Collegiate Church of St. Quentin, had been called "arte canendi clarissimus infantulus." In 1486 Josquin became a singer in the Sistine Chapel choir. These facts are of particular significance because Josquin was the first real genius among the Netherlands masters, and without fear of radical error one might deduce from the fluent vocal character of his compositions that he was a singer with a fine appreciation and mastery of pure legato style.

Josquin was himself the instructor of several important masters, of whom none was more prominent in the advancement of the *a cappella* art than Nicolas Gombert, of Bruges, a singer in the chapel of Charles V and master of the choir from 1530 to 1534. Subsequently he went to Spain with twenty singers, doubtless trained by himself, and became an official of the Imperial chapel in Madrid. Gombert was an ardent cultivator of secular composition. In the pursuit of this branch of his art he developed remarkable descriptive effects and methods of characterization. Indirectly these advances gave to his music and to those of his successors a charming variety which was lacking in the religious works of the time. The cultivation of part singing by all classes of people, which was carried on in this period, made the composer of the madrigal a welcome visitor among the cultured nobility of Italy and France. Gombert wrote often of pastoral delights, with imitations of singing birds, the love lyrics of shepherds and shepherdesses and the terror of the always imminent wolf. He wrote such songs as "Le Chant des Oiseaux," the "Joyeux verger" and "En ce mois delicieux," of which the titles suggest to us the whole world so elegantly depicted in later years by Rousseau.

Clement Jannequin, the famous composer of "Les Cris de Paris" and another "Le Chant des Oiseaux," which have been sung in New York at the concerts of the Schola Cantorum, was probably a pupil of Josquin and certainly a follower of Gombert in the department of secular music. He was also in all likelihood at one time a singer in the Sistine Chapel choir. He lived in the middle of the sixteenth century.

Whether the great Adrian Willaert (1480-1562) was a pupil of Josquin is not quite certain. But he was a singer. For a time he was cantor to a Bohemian king and in 1527 he was made chapel master of St. Mark's in Venice, in which city he founded a singing school. From that institution issued a line of important masters, including Zarlino and Cyprian di Rore, successor of Willaert at St. Mark's.

We are now in the presence of singers, teachers and composers—for every great master of that time was all three—whose influence made itself felt in the dawn of the modern lyric drama. Jacopo Peri, who composed the music of "Euridice" (1600), usually cited as the parent Italian opera, was born in Florence in 1561 and studied music under Cristofano Malvezzi of Lucca. Malvezzi, born in 1547, was in 1571 a canon in the church of St. Lorenzo in Florence and on the death of Corteccia succeeded him as maestro di cappella to the Grand Duke of Tuscany. This means that he was a singer and a master of voice. Corteccia, whom Malvezzi succeeded, was born at Arezzo early in the sixteenth century and died in 1571. In 1539 he became maestro di cappella to Cosimo I, which signifies, of course, that he was a vocal master of the foremost rank.

It is not essential to the purpose of this book to follow this line of investigation into further detail. The fact that the leading musicians of the fruitful years of the thirteenth, fourteenth, fifteenth and sixteenth centuries were not only composers of vocal music, but also singers and instructors of singers is established. The unbroken line of descent of the art of song is from the schools of Pope Julian, founded in 314, to the period immediately preceding the birth of modern Italian opera is thus broadly, but clearly traced. With Claudio Monteverdi, the first musical genius who wrote for the lyric stage of Italy, we meet a composer who was not a singer.

He was a violist, an iconoclast in harmony and an explorer in instrumentation.

What has been set forth about the teaching of vocal art shows us that the singers of the first lyric dramas were trained in exactly the same way as the choristers of the church were. However, we naturally inquire whence came the women singers whom we find in the enjoyment of a full blaze of glory at the close of the sixteenth century. The search after their predecessors will involve us in a general review of the spread of singing among the people.

It has been shown that the troubadours were among the earliest, if they were not the first, secular singers who possessed vocal training. It is not probable that all of them had studied singing, yet those of the nobility (and almost all of them were of that class) certainly had the opportunity to do so when receiving their education in the abbeys.

Almost upon the heels of the troubadours came the cantori a liuto with a class of lyrics which became familiar in all classes of Italian society, but were especially favored by the more cultivated. In the Vatican there is a poem by one Lemmo of Pistoja with the note "Casella diede il suono." This Casella was well known. He was born in 1300 and among other things he wrote music for Dante's sonnet "Amor nella mente." There can hardly be any question that he was a singer to the lute. These lutenists and singers habitually composed in simple polyphony and after giving the melody to the voice arranged the other parts so that they formed a supporting harmony and could be performed on the lute. The whole subject of the cantore a liuto is treated elaborately by Ambros in his "Geschichte der Musik." We need go no further here than is necessary to satisfy ourselves that the practice of singing songs of romantic character survived the era of the troubadours, which was ended about the middle of the thirteenth century, and that it existed so long afterward that its methods were adopted in the preparation of the solo parts of the first secular lyric drama, the "Orfeo" of Angelo Poliziano, produced in Mantua about 1474. For an exhaustive examination of this work the author refers the reader to his "Some Forerunners of Italian Opera" (New York, Henry Holt & Co., 1911).

Bocaccio wrote the stories of his "Decameron" in the years from 1348 to 1358, and in them we find a vivacious representation of social life, in which singing appears to hold an accepted position. To the music of the song "Io son si vaga della mia bellezza" the company dances and we are thus offered a clear picture of the ballata or dance song. Again Emilia invites Dioneo to sing a canzona. Still again Dioneo with a lute and Fiametta with a viol play a dance and yet again one of the company sings while Dioneo accompanies her on the lute.

Singing among such an assembly as Boccacio paints may indeed have been largely of the "natural" type, but the probabilities are that it presupposed a certain amount of cultivation. The practice of instrumental music, which he brings to our notice, seems to indicate that there had been some study and we are further persuaded to regard music as a polite accomplishment by the fact that the entire tendency of the time was toward polyphonic composition. The period of the last troubadours and the earliest cantori a liuto was that in which the great polyphonic art of northern Europe was assuming definite form and there is no question that long before the art of the lute singer had yielded to the splendors of the madrigal drama all the songs of the cantori were adapted from part music. This was the more easily accomplished after the frottola became a well-defined Italian form. This kind of part song was harmonized in simple manner, its stanzas were strophic and its melody facile. The common people of Italy sang their frottole in harmonized parts just as the Russians and Welsh of later centuries sang their folk songs. In a collection published by Petrucci in 1509 there is a frottola by Tromboncino, the most famous master of this species of song, and an arrangement of it for solo voice and lute by Franciscus Bossinensis. In a play of 1539 with music by Corteccia we find a solo for Silenus, a madrigal arranged for one voice and accompaniment of instruments on exactly the same fundamental plan as the lutenists used. But in this case we have the four parts fully developed, the melody being sung and the other three played. Castiglione called this kind of singing "recitar alla lira."

Of the spread of part singing through Europe we have abundant testimony. In the fifteenth century it was practised by all classes and choral societies were more numerous than they were in modern Germany. From the Netherlands the art spread southward into Italy, and we read with delight the story of Lorenzo the Magnificent issuing forth in the nights of the carnival season with a numerous body of followers and making the air ring with music. In the introduction to a collection of "Triumph and Carnival Songs" published in Florence in 1559 Il Lasca says: "Thus they traversed the city singing to the accompaniment of music arranged for four, eight, twelve or even fifteen voices supported by various instruments."

We need not, however, confine ourselves to Italy in our survey of the spread of cultivated song. England was for no inconsiderable period in the van of the advance. Erasmus, who died in 1536, wrote: "The English challenge the prerogative of having the handsomest women, of keeping the best table, and of being the most accomplished in the skill of music of any people." The ladies of Elizabeth's court could read at sight, and accompany themselves on lutes or other instruments. Henry VIII, originally intended for a priest, studied music as a matter of course. Anne Bullen was an enthusiast about the compositions of Josquin des Pres. Edward VI impressed the French ambassador in 1551 by playing the lute. An educated gentleman of this time was expected to be able to sing at sight and even to be acquainted with the art of descant, so that he could improvise a part on a given melody. Musical instruments were at hand everywhere, even for those in the barber shops awaiting the welcome note of "Next." And as Chappell notes, "Tinkers sang catches, milkmaids sang ballads, carters whistled; each trade, and even the beggars, had their special songs." *

In 1529 Elena, daughter of Pietro Bembo, the famous cardinal and littérateur, wrote a letter (still extant) to her father asking permission to take lessons on the monochord (a precursor of the piano) and his answer goes to show that the study of instrumental music was no great novelty among girls of social position, though not yet in high favor.

Just when the professional women singers made their debut on the highway of vocal progress is extremely difficult to determine. One thing, however, is certain, namely, that they must have flourished long before 1600, for at that time there were several of great fame and there existed already exercises for female voices.

* Read H. E. Krehbiel's "Pianoforte and its Music," Chapter V.

CHAPTER VI

APPROACH OF THE MONODIC STYLE

THAT a certain appreciation of the expressive power of the solo voice, or at least an enjoyment of its comparatively free utterance, existed during the years when the polyphonic method of composition was approaching its highest development is evident. The ecclesiastic writers were the scholars and their art was the product of intense concentration upon the technical resources of vocal composition. But even while the people of Italy were singing part songs, the charm of a predominant melody, to which other parts were subject, made itself felt. The influence of folk music could never be completely abolished, and in those singular contrapuntal pieces in which secular songs were employed as counterpoint to chants its battle for recognition was carried on in an extraordinary manner.

The revolution effected by the young coterie of Florentines in the final years of the sixteenth century was not the sudden outburst of a creative genius so much as it was the seizure of existing materials and the deliberate application of them to a clearly defined artistic purpose. Throughout the slow advance toward the Italian opera we can without difficulty trace a steady movement toward the elevation of a single-voiced melody to the throne of vocal art and the crowning of the high voice as the royalty of singing.

We may at this point call into court a witness whose scholarship entitles his conclusions, drawn from systematic research, to the utmost respect. Guido Gasperini, librarian of the conservatory of Parma, writing in the "Encyclopédie de la Musique" on the music of Italy in the fourteenth and fifteenth centuries, directs our attention to the continued tendency of fifteenth century composers in their frottole and strambotti to allot to the highest voice the most expressive part of the composition. From this he draws the conclusion that in many cases, though not in all, the composition was intended to be sung by the upper voice, while the other voice parts were to be performed on instruments, or at any rate an instrument capable of polyphonic utterance, as, for example, the lute.

In the opinion of Signor Gasperini this characteristic gives the music of the fifteenth century a particular significance. Analysis of numerous works shows that composers allotted to the soprano the sustained melody, written in a simple fluent cantilena, while the more florid parts were given to the other voices. The melody ascends or descends without hazardous leaps or perilous roulades. The task of the singer is made easy by the absence of passages of difficult intonation and by the clarity of the cantilena.

"It is easy to see," says the author, "that this part was composed for dilettante singers who did not possess the brilliant qualities of professional artists." On the other hand the musicians did not spare the other voices, especially the middle ones, for which they wrote, fearlessly and with luxurious floridity. The style, cultivated in such music as Signor Gasperini has pointed out, and as the author of the present volume has noted in "Some Forerunners of Italian Opera," laid the foundations upon which Peri, Caccini and their confrères began the structure of Italian opera, when they sought to retire complicated polyphony in favor of a simple and direct solo utterance and to condense all the voice parts, except that delivering the melody, in their newly contrived thorough bass.

We shall obtain a clearer view of the move-

ment of the fifteenth and sixteenth century part
song toward solo utterance, and of the growing
prominence of the soprano voice, if we scrutinize
a little more closely the character of the secular
compositions. While the soprano part was written in the simple style already described, the alto
and tenor parts were handled without reserve.

Composers apparently concerned themselves
little with the natural range of these voices, but
sent them scurrying up and down through leaps
and passages which find no resemblance in the
utterance of the principal voice. Often they
pushed them above the soprano, evidently without
fear that its calmly flowing melody would be
obscured in the mass of harmony. This absence
of reserve and the difference of character between
the principal part and the others strengthens the
belief that these songs were intended for solo
voice accompanied by instruments.

Signor Gasperini invites our attention to the
feeble tone of the instruments of the time. The
lute, the harp and the clavier spoke in very soft
accents and composers could at their pleasure
write the voice part low without fear of its being
covered. The basses, too, of the pieces have
little of the melodic character of true polyphony,
but a strongly marked movement which suggests

their fitness for performance on the plucked instruments of the day.

It is probable that the great number of songs composed by the Italian masters of the fifteenth century were written for a solo voice and designed to be accompanied by an instrument of the lute or guitar family. This supposition makes comprehensible the great revolution which was accomplished in the closing years of the sixteenth century, when the Florentine adventurers supplanted polyphony with monodic song. The revolution created nothing new. Its style was nothing else than the ancient popular style of Italy, ignored by the scholars of the polyphonic school, yet sustaining its healthy existence in the frottole and canzonette of the Italian singers. It needed only the authority of the coterie of artists which met at the Palazzo Bardi to bring the old style back to consideration and to invest it with dignity. That the young artists judged this Italian creation to be a reincarnation of the ancient musical language of the Greeks gave it the necessary place in the general estimation and enabled it to supplant the polyphonic music.

The leaning of the Italians toward the use of the solo voice was not determined clearly in the early years of the sixteenth century, but that it existed is made plain to us by a passage in Baldassare Castiglione's famous work "Il Libro del Cortigiano." He is speaking of the tendencies of the court of Urbino, to which he was attached in 1506. He says:

"Messire Frederick answers that the canto a libro (vocal descant), well executed, seems to him beautiful music; but song accompanied by the viol seems more beautiful, because in this species of music almost all the sweetness of the song consists entirely in the voice of one alone, and one hears and appreciates with the greatest attention the manner of the singer and the air, inasmuch as the ear is occupied in following only one voice and every little error is observed, which does not happen when one sings in company, for then one aids the other."

The motive ascribed to the distinguished Duke of Urbino was not generous, to be sure, but his words indicate that even an amateur of respectable attainments yearned for the direct publication of an independent melody.

If we cross the border to glance for a moment at the creations of the French masters about this time, we shall find certain lines even more clearly drawn, especially if we inspect the methods of the composers of the Renaissance period. Here we meet with music polyphonic in structure, but built upon characteristic French melodies, and with a system of part writing which pointed not so directly as the Italian toward the accompanied solo, but which none the less indicated the approaching supremacy of the voice engaged in delivering the melody. Marin Mersenne in his "Harmonie Universelle" (1627) laid down some of the principles of part writing observed in his day.

"The perfection of harmony consists in four part writing. The bass proceeds by the slowest movement among the four. It is not ordinarily written so much in diminutions as the other parts and moves often in thirds, fourths, fifths and octaves, in order to give room to the other parts, especially the uppermost, which should sing in closely joined progressions as much as possible. The tenor should particularly govern the mode and make the cadences in their proper places. The tenor ought to use the most elegant passages in order to embellish the song and entertain the listeners."

Although Mersenne published his work in 1627, his retrospective view naturally included the art as it was practised years before that. We can discern in works of French masters immediately

preceding his time a practice in some respects
similar to that which he describes, and at any
rate we see the employment of the soprano voice

as the singer of the melody and the other voices as creators of the polyphony. A chanson of Claude Lejeune (p. 84), who lived in the second half of the sixteenth century, will serve to illustrate. To give the whole work would occupy too much space, because it consists of a series of couplets, of which the first is delivered by the soprano voice solo. The second introduces the cotralto, the third is in three-part harmony, introducing the tenor, and the fourth in four parts, adding the bass. After each couplet the quartet sings a refrain. A couplet sung by the four voices discloses the entire content of the composition.

As we approach the promotion of dramatic secular music to leadership in the forward march of the tonal art, we discover an apparently·sudden advance of human expression to a position of power. It is, therefore, advisable that we should give some brief consideration to this "gift of tongues," which was destined in the future to make vocal music the most potent, eloquent and far reaching of all forms of composition. Instrumental music was in its infancy when the·modern opera was born, and although it rose to the levels of Beethoven and Brahms, while the opera sank to the decadence of the pre-Wagnerian period, the voice remained and still remains the supreme musical instrument, never faultless in technic, but most eloquent of all in expression. That we may take a just view and have a clear understanding of the limited expressiveness of early song and opera, we must briefly glance at the conditions under which it was developed.

The music of the early chant was without two of the most important elements of musical expression, namely, harmony and rhythm. A vague, formless melody was its sole possession, and its development continued to be purely melodic for more than 800 years. And this melodic development did not include rhythm, as we understand it, until mensural notation had made its influence dominant.

Why were these expressive elements so slow in their rise to importance? Because the church chant aimed to be as impersonal as possible. Its purpose was religious; its moods devotional and contemplative; its musical character intentionally vague and colorless.

When the first solo chanters mounted the ambon, clad in their silken robes and with their long hair falling upon their shoulders, they entered upon the florid elaboration of melody without any thought of the possibilities of expression, but with minds intent upon the achievement of personal glorification. That florid singing without words was praised by St. Augustine and others as a method of expressing such religious ecstasies of uplifted souls as text could not convey, must be accepted as the view of hearers to whom the naïve utterances of an infant art were as the wisdom proceeding out of the mouths of babes and sucklings. But even to-day with all our modern sophistication, all our intimate acquaintance with the tremendous forces of the dramatic dissonance and the modern orchestra, we still confess the suitability of the ecclesiastic floridity to the publication of the rapt state of a mind lost in religious contemplation.

The early chant made no effort at the tender expression possible in a pure cantilena. This sort of cantilena dwelt among the songs of the people. It was a means at that time of small expression, to be sure, but it differed radically from the chant in that it did give voice to purely human feeling. Tragedy, of course, was not yet to be thought of. The musical materials for the embodiment of the tragic passions were unborn. Without immense variety of rhythm and the highest skill in the use of the dissonance the tragic music drama is impossible. Early secular song, in which human feeling, as distinguished from religious abstraction or devotion, was embodied, accomplished nothing larger in the field of expression than the publication of tender pathos.

Plaintive lyrics we find in profusion; but passionate song not at all. For many years after its birth the young lyric drama achieved nothing beyond this.

The secular songs of the ninth century which have come down to us are absolutely without musical expressiveness. Without danger of falling into serious error we may regard all vocal music before that of the troubadours as devoid of clear human communication, and even in the lyrics of the knightly singers we must not seek for too much. Pierre Aubry has summarized his views on this point very plainly:

"What we must not expect to find in medieval music, particularly that of the troubadours and trouvères, is all that subsequent progress and development have added since the time of Saint Louis. But what still lives and counts in this music is the naïveté and grace of youth. The melodic ideas of the troubadours and trouvères are simple, and their means of expression humble. But the ideas are charming and we can listen to them with pleasure. I have spoken of the poverty of their rhythmical formulas, but have hardly done justice to the variety of effects made possible to the composers by the multiplicity of scales; modern music, mostly concerned·with major and

minor scales, has in this respect fewer resources.
Though there is a certain nobility in the troubadour melodies worthy of imitation, the rhythmic
scheme is less satisfactory; it gives us no free
speech in music, but brings us too near the
formalities of Adam, Herold, Boildieu, the 'Dame
Blanche,' 'Zampa,' the 'Chalet'—in fact, the type
of opera popular in the sixties. I would 'almost
venture on the formula—no better and no worse
than all formulæ which claim to summarize an
aesthetic judgment—that a troubadour or trou-
vère melody is of equal value with an air out of
an old fashioned comedy opera sung without an
accompaniment."

The "naïveté and grace of youth" survived
until the secular song succumbed to the influence
of over cultivation. Even then some of the highly
finished madrigals retain something of the earlier
spontaneity, as in the case of Orlando Lasso's
familiar "Matona mia cara." The sentimental
gallantries of the age of chivalry, which animated
the troubadour songs, were succeeded by the
equally sentimental utterances of the cinquecento.
But of the grand passions there could be no publication.

The expressive powers of vocal music remained
within these narrow confines, as we have already

noted, long after the advent of opera. We must, therefore, be convinced that singing continued to be pure legato with all its accessories, while anything approaching strongly accented declamation was not to be found till a later period. The modern art of vocal coloring was unkown. Turbulent emotions were disclosed in a bravura of agitated character, such as survived in Handel's day in the second part of "But who may abide."

We are now prepared for a general survey of the state of singing at the close of the 16th and beginning of the 17th century.

CHAPTER VII

Birth of Dramatic Recitative

At the moment when the young Florentines began their experiments in the field of simplified solo song, which led them to the creation of the modern opera, the musical wealth of Italy possessed a value and an extent too easily underestimated. The music of the church was chiefly ornate polyphony; the chant was decorated with prolonged vocal flourishes, in which the form and spirit of the ancient jubili were preserved. This species of chant was not without its effect on the young explorers of the dramatic world, and their operas contain many pages of recitative constructed upon precisely the same musical lines as those found in these solemn intonations of the sanctuary.

Side by side with this ecclesiastic music flourished the secular song, which was written in the madrigal and allied forms, sung sometimes by four or five voices, sometimes by only one, with the other parts played on instruments. This secular music enjoyed a vigorous life in the madrigal drama, and the works of Orazio Vecchi, the foremost master of this school, battled long with the new "drama per musica" for the supremacy. We have traced the movement of this latter type of music toward solo utterance, but the records which have come down to us prove that the solo singing of madrigals eventually became the field for the most brilliant and dazzling displays of virtuosity.

We find, then, the old type of chant with its undulating final cadence and the new species of solo with its quite modern fiorituri coexisting as the principal kinds of vocal music in which the individual singer was permitted to address himself to the listener. At the same time there were numerous vocalists of amazing skill in florid song, the technic of singing was practically all known, though not perfectly codified, and the way was prepared for the step into the dramatic world.

One thing was still lacking and it continued to be so for some years, namely, the expression of tragic passion. The comments of those who heard early singers disclose the fact that nothing more than the tender pathos already described was within their reach.

We shall better comprehend the state of singing

at the close of the sixteenth century if we refresh
our memories of the developments of the lyric
drama from its advent in the "Orfeo" of Angelo
Poliziano down to the elaborate madrigal dramas
which held the stage at the moment when the
Florentine reformers began their experiments.
The departure of the musical play from the
straight and narrow path indicated by Poliziano
was made in pursuit of spectacular splendors
which appealed with irresistible force to the
luxurious Italian mind. The festival plays produced in the sixteenth century contained pictorial
features of astonishing character, while the music
showed a clearly defined movement away from
the approach to Hellenic declamation found in
the "Orfeo" toward the polyphonic style, either
with several vocal parts, or with a single voice
delivering the melody while instruments played
the other parts.

As early as 1488 Bergonza Botta of Tortoni,
prepared for the marriage of Galeazzo Sforza and
Isabella of Arragon a series of scenes, animated
sketches, ranging from the story of Jason to that
of Orpheus and ending with a ballet in which
Bacchus, Silenus, and Pan were the principal
figures. The Milanese historiographer Tristan
Chalco calls it "the most splendid and astonishing

spectacle that Italy had witnessed." Mercury, Diana and Orpheus sang solos, which were in the inevitable madrigal form with the subsidiary parts given to instruments.

Numerous adulatory spectacles of this sort were produced, notably the two introduced among the festivities at the marriage of Cosimo I and Eleanora of Toledo. The music was composed by Francesco Corteccia, Constanzo Festa, Mattio Rampollini, Pietro Masconi and Baccio Moschini. In one of these plays was the madrigal for voice and instruments reproduced in Kiesewetter's "Schicksale und Beschaffenheit des Weltlichen Gesanges." Whether this madrigal was subjected to the elaborate ornamentation of the singer we do not know, but we have the record of a later decoration.

In 1589 at the marriage in Florence of the Grand Duke Ferdinand with the Princess Christina of Loraine there was a festival entertainment under the direction of the Count of Vernio, at whose palace the Florentine founders of opera were wont to meet. The play was his own "Amico Fido," which was interspersed with six spectacular intermezzi with music by various composers. Kiesewetter reproduces three of them, one sung by Jacopo Peri, composer of the famous

"Euridice," another composed by Emilio del Cavalieri and sung by Onofrio Galfreducci, and the third by Antonio Archilei and sung by his

wife Vittoria. The ornamentation of this madrigal by the singer has been preserved. It is
quoted here from Kiesewetter's "Schicksale und
Beschaffenheit des Weltlichen Gesanges."

It was against this kind of song that the Florentine reformers set their faces, perhaps not with
complete success, for we are told that Mme.
Archilei decorated the music of Euridice in much
the same manner. But nevertheless two distinct
purposes were set forth by the young adventurers, namely, to make the texts intelligible to
the listener and to impart direct human expression
to vocal music. Our clearest information comes
from Caccini's preface to his "Nuove Musiche."
He says:

"When I now see many of these pieces torn
apart and altered in form, when I see to what
evil use the long runs are put, to wit, those
consisting of single and double notes, (repeated
ones), as if both kinds were combined, and which
were invented by me in order to do away with
the former old fashion of introduced passages,
which were for wind or stringed instruments
rather than the human voice; when further I see
how dynamic gradations of tone are used without
discrimination, what enunciation now is, how
trills, gruppetti and other ornaments are intro-

duced, I consider it necessary—and in this I am upheld by my friends—to have my music printed."

Caccini further informs us that his life among men of culture in Florence had brought him much wise counsel and valuable experience, which urged him "to place no value upon that music which makes it impossible to understand the words and thus to destroy the unity and meter, sometimes lengthening the syllables, sometimes shortening them in order to suit the counterpoint —a real mangling of the poetry—but to hold fast to that principle so greatly extolled by Plato and other philosophers: 'Let music be first of all language and rhythm, and secondly tone.' "

Then came to him the idea of a style of music "which makes it possible in a certain manner to speak musically by employing, as already said, a certain noble subordination of the song, with now and then some dissonances, while however holding the chord by means of the sustained bass" and so on.

Caccini's artistic aims are indisputable. He strove to strike off the shackles of counterpoint in all its forms, whether the elaborately written polyphony of the old madrigals or the still surviving type of *contrapunctus a mente*, preserved

in the fiorituri of Archilei and her kind. Freed
from such entanglements, song was to subor-
dinate itself to a simple, expressive setting of the
text. That we find in the declamation of the
first operas no tumultuous utterance of human
passion is not astonishing. This new art was the
product of minds steeped in the Hellenic studies
of the Renaissance. The young Florentines had
in mind a resuscitation of the Greek declamation,
and the people of their dramas intoned their utterances with a half divine smoothness and dignity
which irresistibly brings to our minds the character of the Greek sculpture.

Caccini, however, was not averse to the use
of florid melody when it suited his dramatic purpose. Three short excerpts from his "Euridice"
may be quoted, the first to show the style of his
newly introduced recitative, the second a florid
passage, and the third his treatment of the voices
of two nymphs in a manner afterward found in
many hundreds of pages of Italian opera (p. 100).

Here then let us pause, for the temptation to
linger amid the splendors of this period is great.
It is a period crowded with personages of fame
and power; of artists celebrated, capricious, consummate in skill, wayward in manners; of
princely patrons and cultured publics. History

has long entitled the Handelian era "the golden age of bel canto," but if perhaps the sun of vocal virtuosity attained its high noon in Handel's day, it rose in its most bewildering glory in the first years of the seventeenth century. By the end of that cycle certainly the vocal virtuoso had reached a position quite equal to that enjoyed by Caffarelli and Farinelli, and we may dwell with delight upon the pregnant history of the time. We must first

man - - - - -

- - - - ti'I so - le.

val mor - tal in - ge - - - - gno

gia non val mor - tal in - ge - - gno

examine the knowledge of technic as handed down to us by such masters as Caccini, Zacconi and Bovicelli, and view the achievements of the eminent singers whose art antedated that of the idols of London in the early eighteenth century.

CHAPTER VIII

WHAT THE EARLY MASTERS TAUGHT

OUR knowledge of the technic of singing at the close of the sixteenth and during the seventeenth centuries is derived from the works of theorists and teachers whose writings are neither difficult of access nor obscure in style. The most important are these:

Giovanni Battista Bovicelli, "Regole di Musica" and "Madrigali e Motetti Passaggiati," both published in 1594. The dates of the author's birth and death are uncertain, but it is clear that he was a distinguished teacher of singing in the last years of the sixteenth century.

Giulio Caccini (1560?-1615?) "Nuove Musiche" (1601) and in other works chiefly those of Doni and del Valle, who recorded some of his teachings.

Ludovico Zacconi, born in the middle of the sixteenth century. The date of his death is unknown. His great work, completed about 1619, was entitled "Prattica di Musica utile et necessaria si al compositore si anco al cantare." Chapters 38-40 treat of solmization; 48-56, rules for singers with many exercises; 67-71, duties of maestra di capella and singers: 74-80, mutual qualifications of composers and singers.

Johann Crüger (1598-1662). "Preceptae Musicae Practicae Figuralis" (1625). Also in a German version (1660) "Rechter Weg zur Singekunst."

Johann Andreas Herbst (1588-1666). "Musica Practica sive Instructo pro Symphoniacis" (1642).

Francesco Severi (—— 1630). "Salmi Passaggiati" (1615).

Benigne de Bacilly (about 1625-1692). "Remarques Curieuses sur l'Art de Bien Chanter" (1668).

The Frenchman mentioned last made some serious efforts toward systematic treatment of French vowel sounds, but aside from that followed the Italians as closely as possible. Herbst and Crüger, the two German masters, were professors of the Italian method of their time. Bovicelli and Caccini appear to have left us the most satisfactory records of the teaching of the period which may be thus outlined:

1. The pupil must first of all things know and understand the text and endeavor to interpret it.

2. Long study of solfeggi was necessary for this. The student must work the voice on six tones in moderate force, and without any haste in the direction of voice extension.

3. First studies in voice were called "accenti" (to be explained later) and these were followed by short diminutions and the various ornaments, especially the slow "tremolo" (shake).

4. "Esclamazio" and swell tone, which equalized the registers and also imparted life to the style. These will be explained later.

5. Accompaniments were not used in lessons in order that the pupil might acquire certainty of intonation through independence.

6. Two and three voiced solfeggi were much used. They were held to be good for attack, rhythm and voice extension.

7. Agility of voice was sought, but only a moderate colorature was regarded as desirable. Beauty of tone was never sacrificed. On the contrary, it was the first requisite.

In their consideration of the treatment of text the old masters gave serious and intelligent attention to the characters of the vowel sounds. In the preface to his "Daphne" Marco da Gagliano says that clear articulation of the syllables in order to make the words intelligible should "always be the chief aim of the singer in every kind of song, especially recitative." Herbst declares that from youth the singer should practise "in voce et pronunciatione articulata." Doni, Bovicelli and the rest give similar precepts. These teachers divided the vowels into open and closed, the open being A and O, the closed I and U (the Italian sounds, of course). Zarlino sternly forbids any alteration of the sounds. Durante* noted the proper position of the mouth, it being naturally more open for the open vowels than for the closed. Caccini writes of the same matter and speaks of the greater sonority of the open vowels. Herbst and Crüger also say that the position of the mouth should be governed by the vowel sound. The masters in general began with exercises sung on the open vowels. The closed were introduced later.

The first aims of these teachers were to insure correct intonation and to make their pupils sing musically. The groundwork of the pupils' training was the "accentus," which was the root form

---

*Ottavio Durante: Arie Devote, le quale in se contegnono la maniera di cantar con gratia l' imitatione delle parole et il modo di sonar passaggi et altri affetti. Rome, 1608.

of the diminution. It differed from the diminution not in character, but in quantity. The diminution was merely that common form of variation which transforms a simple melody into a running passage by breaking it up into shorter notes. Here is an "accentus" as found in Crüger's work:

Ut, re, mi, fa, so la.

Ut,   re,   mi,   fa,   sol.   la.

The accentus was used also to give the pupil a smooth legato. After the accentus the masters taught the tremolo, gruppo and trillo. Finally came "passages" and complete coloratura. The accentus was taught first on six tones of the scale, as shown in the example just given. No attempt was made at extension of the scale till the exercises within this hexachord could be correctly sung. Extension was then made carefully with two tones upward and one downward. Everything was sung with moderate force and slowly. Nothing about power can be found in the teachings of the old masters. The volume of tone was permitted to develop naturally. The teacher and the student concerned themselves only with correctness, which meant perfect intonation, pure vowel sounds and flowing smooth delivery. The range used in these extension exercises was from E to G or D to F for a high voice and correspondingly lower for low voices. When the new tones were introduced they were always shorter than those already developed.

Nothing was ever done which could impose the least strain on the singer. Everything was to be done slowly. We find Bovicelli, Zacconi and Donati insisting on this and Zacconi in particular warns against practising with a large tone. Increase in tempo was allowed when the accenti could be sung perfectly at a slow pace. Pupils were taught to sing piano with a vibrant tone, not a hollow one. The masters were not entirely agreed as to the use of vowels in solfeggi. Zacconi advocated teaching all the sounds, open and closed, from the beginning; Caccini believed in using only the open ones. But all agreed that voice cultivation should begin in the middle, and that extension should be made only when this part could be correctly used. This practice was lost in the eighteenth century, but is now generally in use again

After such scale fragments as those shown in the Crüger exercise the old masters began to give their pupils work in intervals. Caccini advocated the use of the third as a beginning—the second having already been acquired in the scale fragments of the accenti. Some teachers used ascending thirds, others descending. Caccini declared that no rule could be made. However, he showed a preference for the employment of ascending thirds. He says that the upper tone must be derived from the lower by "a slow swelling." The expression is somewhat obscure, but not unintelligible. He felt that a good intonation could be obtained better by rising than falling thirds.

The "esclamazio," upon which Caccini and several others laid so much stress, was a device intended to heighten the expressiveness of song. Its technical basis, as will be seen, was a perfect command of the breath. The device was a combination of diminuendo and crescendo, somewhat mechanically formed, but to be used only where the text suggested it. In the beginning of his experiments with the esclamazio Caccini favored a strong attack followed by a diminution of tone and at the close of the phrase a slight crescendo. He declared that a little increase of breath when the tone was diminishing made it more expressive. This device appears in two forms as follows:

Esclamazio languida $< > <$

Esclamazio viva $> <$

The difference between the characters of these two devices is at once manifest. The former was suited to broader phrases than the latter. In fact the esclamazio viva was not recognized as a fundamental factor in the delivery of tragic recitative. On the other hand in the singing of canzone the viva was freely employed.

Caccini warns that in these uses of crescendo and diminuendo there must be no forcing of the voice. Only the mezzo forte was reached. The swell tone, or "messa di voce," was the increase and diminution of voice on a single note, and at a later period, as shown by the teachings of some eighteenth century masters, the messa di voce was to be used on all long tones, no matter what the sense of the text. This was a diametrical departure from the artistic ideals of Caccini and his contemporaries. Domenico Mazzochi (1590-1650) in his "Madrigali a cinque voci" gives particular directions for the use of the swell tone, using the same signs as we use to-day. He also employs the letter C. Ignacio Donati, who flourished in the beginning of the seventeenth century, tells us that the esclamazio should be sung broadly and reposefully. The singer was allowed great latitude in its delivery in regard to time and its modifications. He made his own ritardandi and accelerandi. Durante gives us the same information.

It will be clear to singers that the esclamazio was a comprehensive device which embraced not only certain technical features, but the basis of expression by tonal nuance. Technically it was an exercise of the first importance in breath control; and, as it included management of the breath in phrases of some extent and range, it was also a means of equalizing registers. In this latter office it resembled some of the exercises recommended in our own time by the younger Lamperti. Its signficance in the department of vocal expression need hardly be described, since every singer of this day knows the value of a perfect command of graded dynamics. Here are two examples of the esclamazio (p. 111).

These are taken from Caccini's "Nuove Musiche" and the technical marks are those given by Goldschmidt. The first tone in the second example has the direction "diminish the voice." The expression "crescere e scemare la voce" was

equivalent to "messa di voce" or swell tone. This swell could be carried from pianissimo to fortissimo and back, but it is improbable that a singer would attack the "Deh" in the quoted madrigal at full voice. In the esclamazio languida the customary range of dynamics extended from pianissimo to forte, back to pianissimo and thence up again to mezzo forte. In the esclamazio viva the range was from forte to pianissimo and up again to mezzo forte.

Caccini taught the esclamazio immediately after the accenti, a fact which shows that he regarded it as one of the fundamental elements of voice development, as well as of style.

This brings us to a consideration of the views of the early masters in regard to registers. One finds in Cerone's "Il Melopeo" (1613) information about the knowledge of registers in his time, but more explicit propositions are those laid down by the teachers, especially Caccini. This master recognized two registers, chest and head, which he called "voce piena" and "voce finte." From his writings it becomes clear that by chest register he meant all the tones now called chest and medium. It is therefore more precise to speak of Caccini's two registers as natural and head. These he allowed to women, falsetti and boys. Male voices were to use only the natural and not the head tones. He preferred the natural voice because the head was more difficult to control. It demanded a better management of the breath, which, according to him, was likely to fail just where the singer most needed it. He did not, however, object to a judicious use of head tones. He leaned in practice toward the esclamazio viva, because to increase the power of the tone in passing from head to medium register was often disagreeable, especially in soprano voices.

Caccini knew that forcing the breath led to sharpening of a note. He was also aware that when muscular expansion had reached its limit more breath was needed to reach a higher tone. In the artificial or head register this necessity would arise in the highest tones. With such points in mind he studied the esclamazio as a means of equalizing the registers, because he perceived that this expressive device could not be well sung if the voice showed breaks. In his consideration of the matter he looked into vowel sounds. He asserts that the vowel I is more favorable to a tenor than U, while in the case of sopranos the case is just the opposite. But in general these early teachers exercised voices first on open vowels and later on closed.

Most of the early teachers agree with Caccini as to registers and their use; but Pretorius, Herbst and Crüger forbid the use of head tones for all voices. Perhaps in this characteristically Teutonic attitude we may find a point of departure looking toward the subsequent divergence in the vocal styles of the Latins and the Germans.

CHAPTER IX

THE ORNAMENTS AND PASSAGES

WE come now to a view of ornaments and passages as taught by the old masters. Caccini introduced the ornaments into his courses immediately after the esclamazio. It has already been pointed out that some of the ornaments, such as the trill, were very old, and the basic elements of the seventeenth century system of colorature, known to church singers of the ninth century, were set forth in 1555 in the "Fontegara" of Canassi del Fontego. He indicated fiorituri and diminutions for flute and said that they were also suitable for voices. A conventionalized placing of embroideries on principal and semi-principal cadences was extant in the last years of the sixteenth century. These decorations now began to be used not only on cadences but other parts of the melody. The singer was warned not to embroider semibreves accompanied by text. Nevertheless to content one's self with ornamenting only cadences betrayed one's ignorance and weakness.

Special types of vocalises for different voices

were in use and much time was occupied in acquiring not rapid and brilliant, but smooth and elegant delivery of the various ornaments employed in the art of the period. The terminology of the ornaments underwent many changes. Terms used at one time to signify certain forms, such as trillo or tremolo, were used a little later to signify others, and confusion is likely to arise in the mind of any student who does not observe the dates. But through the last years of the sixteenth and nearly all of the seventeenth century the names of the ornaments were not applied as we apply them. Caccini begins his instruction in ornaments with the trillo, which, he says, should be first undertaken with the broad sound of A. The so-called trill of Caccini's day, however, was not that of our time. Here are two examples, one from Caccini and the other from Herbst:

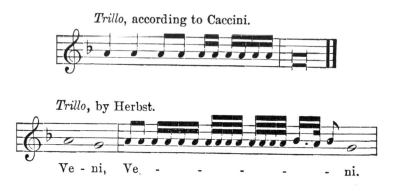

Trillo, according to Caccini.

Trillo, by Herbst.

Ve - ni, Ve - - - - - ni.

The reader will see that this singular figure is something now obsolete. It was sung with an aspiration at the beginning of each note. Tomasso Aceti, a theorist quoted by Baini, the biographer of Palestrina, describes this trillo as "a wavering of the voice with continual aspiration." Manuel Garcia regarded it as a kind of martellato and believed that it required a strong coup de glotte for each tone. This so-called trill was in use in the early years of the eighteenth century. Even Bach and Handel occasionally used it. It was at that time called tremolo.

The ornament known to us as the trill was in Caccini's day called gruppo. Here is the form as given in Caccini's writings:

Gruppo, by Caccini.

This same figure was called tremolo by Herbst and Crüger and was either ascending or descending. Among the Italians and even the French (as we learn from Bacilly) preference was accorded to the ascending form. Herbst and Crüger both give the ornament thus:

Bovicelli distinguishes between grupetti of

Tremolo, according to Herbst and Crüger.
Tremolo ascendens.   *Tremolo descendens.*

notes of equal and unequal values, but this seems
a matter of no technical importance. Herbst believed the tremolo (our trill) the best method
of developing agility; but other masters appear
to have regarded all the ornaments as essential
to this purpose. These teachers began the use
of these ornaments early and used them very
often. Caccini, as we have noted, advocated the
employment of "ah" for trill practice, but Donati
and Zacconi used also E and O. All the teachers
seems to have agreed on the exclusion of I and U.

Caccini, like our modern teachers, gave his
pupils an exercise preparatory to the gruppo
(trill). He called it "rabbattuta di gola," which
is difficult to translate. "Rabbatere," of which
"rabbatutta" is the noun, means to half close and
"gola" means the throat. The figure was this:

Caccini's bitterest complaint in his "Nuove
Musiche" is about the misuse of passages. The

Rabattuta di gola.

passage, or diminution, as we saw in Chapter II, was one of the oldest devices of vocal music, and had come to be lavishly employed without regard for the text. It was the disregard of the text which offended Caccini. The practice had begun in the Papal chapel at least as far back as the ninth century, when the appoggiatura, syncopation, mordent, portamento and other graces of song were used indiscriminately. In the final years of the sixteenth century the church singers freely introduced passages in their polyphonic music, and after the introduction of the dramatic recitative seemed more anxious than ever to make the sanctuary a parade ground for the baroque style which the innovations of Caccini and Peri threatened. In the course of time the attempts to rival instruments in the execution of passages led to the creation of difficulties beyond the powers of singers. But in the seventeenth century we find much of the thought of the teacher directed to the preparation of the pupil for the delivery of florid passages.

The groundwork was laid in the practice of the accenti, already described. The ornaments followed, generally in the order previously mentioned. The method of that time was akin to our own. The singer began with simple vocalises

and advanced by careful gradations to the most
difficult ones. Vocalises were written by all the
leading masters. Cerone gives many in his "Il
Melopeo." Adamo Banchieri, the madrigal drama
composer, wrote 100 vocalises for the four principal voices. His method may be deduced from
a single fragment:

Passage, by Banchieri.

Bovicelli gives the clearest instructions about
the use of passages. He says they should be
employed only where the text permits them and
should always be so constructed that the words
can be understood. The quantities of syllables
must not be changed and a passage begun on any
syllable must continue through it. He says that
the use of ornament must regard the movement
of the other voices and the laws of counterpoint
and harmony. He cautions the singer against
repeating passages in the same rhythm. He
should learn how to vary them by changing the

values of the notes. Bovicelli and Caccini both say that a succession of notes of unequal value is preferable to one of equal notes. All passages must be sung legato; there must be no coup de poitrine. Here are two passages of Bovicelli on a plain chant alleluia:

Passage, by Bovicelli.

The rhythmical changes referred to by Bovicelli were usually left to the taste of the singer and not written. They consisted chiefly in the alteration of successions of notes of equal length into phrases such as this:

That the early music lovers were fond of syncopation is shown by the fact that this form frequently appears:

This syncopation was known as the Lombard figure, and apparently the Italian theorists believed that it originated in the neighborhood of

Milan. It was common in seventeenth century music and even survived till the time of Handel, who (for example) uses it in an air for Delilah in his "Samson." Bovicelli's instructions continue with the warning that there must be no haste in the delivery of passages. The attack and the rhythm must be carefully observed. Colorature must be moderate in pace, not too quick. The tones must be clearly separated so that each one is distinguishable. Apparent ease in delivery, perfect time and rhythm were absolutely essential in colorature. Zacconi lays equal emphasis on this. The old school was decidedly opposed to crackling fireworks. Repose and elegance were demanded.

In regard to the breath the old teachers were not in the least ambiguous. Severi in his "Salmi Passaggiati" says that in delivering passages of semiquavers the singing must be swift and vivacious, but the notes must be continually distinguishable and the separation between them

must be made "dal petto e non dal gola." Goldschmidt, as well as Lemaire and Lavoix, believes
that this means that they are to be sung with the
chest and not the head voice. But it seems more
probable that, when he says the notes are to be
"spiccate" "from the chest and not from the
throat," he means the end is to be reached by
management of the breath and not by muscular
action of the throat.

The rule for the composer, as for the singer,
was that the sense of the text must decide where
passages should be used. But the composers and
singers both broke this rule much too often.
Accenti and passages were to be executed in one
breath. If a passage was composed of notes of
unequal value, it was permitted to take breath
after a long tone. But the masters all urged
pupils to learn how to sing a phrase in one breath
—"far l'habbito di cantarle in un fiato," to quote
Donati's words. Bovicelli demands that singers
shall always think about the breath and complains
sharply about those who "pigliano ad ogni poco
di note il fiato"—take breath every few notes.
Zacconi declares that two things are to be sought
by those who wish to practise the profession of
singing, namely, chest and throat, the former to
supply the power to sing a passage through to

its "giusto termino" (correct conclusion) and the other to furnish the ease in delivery.

Bovicelli objects to the use of the half breath among a succession of quickly moving notes. He declares that it sounds badly and prefers to change the passage so that it can be sung without resort to this device. Finally the taking of the breath must be inaudible. Bovicelli sarcastically remarks that it is very bad to make more sound with the breath than with the voice.

Five years were required by most masters for the training of the pupils. Special vocalises were written by nearly all of these instructors and naturally those produced toward the end of the seventeenth century were more brilliant than the early ones. But the masters continued to require the pupils to vocalize without the aid of instruments in order that certainty in intonation might be acquired. For this purpose many vocalises for two or even three voices were written. We may note two produced toward the close of the century:

Solfeggiamenti a Due Voci, etc., da Giovanni Buonaventura Viviani, Firenze, 1693.

Duo Tessuti con diversi solfeggiamenti, scherzi, etc., dal Signor Giuseppe Giamberti Romano, Rome, 1689.

Giamberti's work is especially interesting because it shows us the classification of voices at
this period. The author makes note of the difference between high and low altos, and includes
male voices (tenors) in the latter class. Whereas
in the first half, and indeed during most of the
seventeenth century, the tenor is never asked to
rise above G, Giamberti gives this voice a range
of 14½ tones from B flat to high B. In the early
years of the century the range of the soprano
voice was what we would now regard as low.
But as the castrati came into prominence the
range of both sopranos and altos was increased
upward. Falsettists and boys went to the upper
G; castrati and women passed above this G to
the upper C and in some cases even to D or E.

Baritones were distinguished from basses, but
indeed though the baritone voice was not treated
as it is now, but rated as a first bass, it was
known and named early in the century. The
title "barytono" appears in "Il Primo Libro de
Madrigaletti a una, due e tre voci," by Biandra
Gio Pietro, Venice, 1626. In this collection appears an air for baritone written on the F clef
on the third line. The general classification of
voices with their ranges as given by the seventeenth century masters was as follows:

The masters had much to say about deportment and hygiene. Zarlino complains of linguistic errors and the absence of dignified bearing on the stage. He advises the student to read his air before singing it in order that he may understand the words and manage the voice accord-

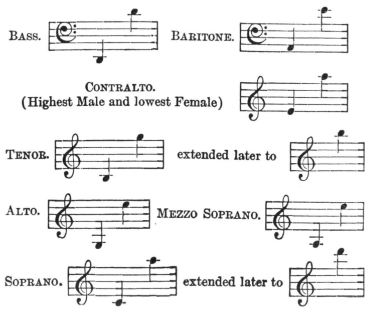

(Contralto and Tenor an octave lower than here written)

ingly. The style must be governed by the meaning of the song and the vowels must not be altered.

Other masters agree with him in advising the student to avoid using much voice in beginning a song in order not to weary the lungs. The

pupils are cautioned not to try to sing too high
or too low. They should eat only light foods,
and avoid almonds, filberts and walnuts, which
dry the "chest." Singers should not eat before
singing, and between closely succeeding appearances only vegetables. Falsetti, soprani and con-
tralti should take only very light wine, because
wine impairs the purity of the voice and imparts
sharpness to it. Tenors and basses, if young,
and above all in the spring, should dilute their
wine because undiluted the wine heats the stomach
and makes the mouth dry. In winter on the contrary one should drink wine just as it comes
from the vine. The old should drink wine
"straight" all the time. A singer should not
write much. The position of the body bent over
a desk or table is very fatiguing for the chest.
Cerone says that this is the reason composers
rarely have good voices. If the singer must write,
let him use a desk at which he can stand.

Many more details of the teachings and practice of the old masters could be given, but the
essentials of the famous Italian method, which
trained the princes of the vocal world, have been
set forth. In considering the achievements of the
singers thus trained we must bear in mind that
volume of tone was not sought and heavy orches-

tration was unknown. There were airs for singers with powerful voices, but usually one instrument, preferably, the trumpet, was employed to establish a standard of comparison. Purcell, Bach and some others wrote such airs; but in the latter years of the seventeenth century the tendency was to reduce the instrumental accompaniment of solos to the smallest proportions in order that nothing might interfere with the public enjoyment of the voice.

Keeping this in mind, we see that normal development of the scale, conservation of force, perfect management of the breath and consummate ease and smoothness in the delivery of passages and ornaments were certain to be attained by the method of these old teachers. Theirs was the true golden age of bel canto, for all that Porpora, Fedi, Pistocchi and their contemporaries knew they owed to the great masters of the early seventeenth century.

CHAPTER X

Male Soprani and Other Virtuosi

We may now return to the historical survey. In our study of this period we shall be obliged from time to time to overstep its limits. No inclusive review of these fruitful years can be made without occasional retrospects of the past and flights beyond the border which separates them from the succeeding era.

When the seventeenth century began, the glory of the virtuoso singer, as we have noted, was already spread above the horizon of musical art. His sun had risen, and by the end of the century it was blazing in the intolerable splendor of its high noon. Our prospect is crowded with composers who were singers, singers who were composers or decorators of other men's compositions, women who rivalled the most famous diva of modern times in their amazing skill in florid song, and whose musicianship was such that some of them rivalled their masculine contemporaries as composers, cardinals who were the princely patrons and in a measure dictators of the realm of music, male sopranos already challenging the attention of the world and claiming that imperial crown which was ultimately set upon their arrogant brows.

The scene is animated, somewhat confused, somewhat difficult of appreciation, because the perspective is so long that this thickly peopled background spreads itself before us in a flat mass of figures which we separate with difficulty. Already, however, we have noted the advent of such artists as Peri and Caccini, composers and singers, who were actively concerned in the birth of the monodic style of the young Florentine school, a style which, as we have seen, was not artificially made, but legitimately descended through an artistic line.

In our view of the secular part song we have seen elements of the new solo style gradually shaping themselves into the monody. We have also found the first advance of the woman's voice to its normal position, and the relegation to singers of the business of filling the outlines left in some parts by the composers.

But the most significant feature of the progress of this time was the lifting into prominence of the individuality of the artist, a thing impossible in the polyphonic era. To the soloist was now gradually given the duty of imparting vitality and human expression to the somewhat cold and stately parlando of the composer. Not only do we read of such famous singers as Peri and Caccini, who wrote operas and other music, but of Vittoria Archilei, the Euridice of Peri's work, Francesca Caccini, daughter of Giulio, herself a celebrated soprano and a composer, Adriana Baroni, and her illustrious daughter Leonora, and Loreto Vittori, the male soprano who bestrode the world of song like a Colossus. Of him there will be more to say later. At present we need note only that after several years in the home of Nicola Doni in Florence, during which time his vocal cultivation was pursued to its completion, he emerged into blazing publicity, so that one of the Donis tells us that he actually introduced a new style of singing in Florence, where the *stile parlante* was born. His fame travelled to Rome and the Cardinal Ludovisi induced Cosimo de Medici to let him go to that city. It was there that he became the intimate friend of Nicias Erythraeus, his biographer, from whom quotations will presently be made. Erythraeus was so deeply moved by Vittori's impersonation in the "Magdalena" of Mazzochi that he caused a statue to be erected to the singer and the character.

Cardinal Ludovisi exercised a monopoly in the gifts of Vittori. It was a delightful custom of Cardinals at that time to own singers. Ludovisi cherished his treasure and permitted only an exclusive society of aristocrats to hear him. His was no art for pebeian ears, declared the ecclesiastic. As in the fifteenth century the passionate sensualism of the Italian mind had revealed itself in the drama and theatrical music, so in the sixteenth it sustained its vitality, but expended its ecstasies upon different objects. In the fifteenth Princes, Dukes, petty nobles, lords of the church and bourgeois adventurers into the region of aristocracy rivalled each other in the spirit of their writings and the luxury of their private entertainments. The comedy, elegant songs, concerts of instruments, glittering ballets, intricate pantomimes, all afforded a field for the employment of the theatrical arts, including astonishing machinery, as well as for imported singers and instrumentalists.

In the seventeenth century the idol of the operatic stage first unveiled himself to these worshippers of the artist, and no prince of the church regarded his train as complete without a soprano, male or female. Rome led the world in the new idolatry. No later than 1626 there was a war of factions in the Holy City. The Cortists valiantly upheld the fame of Margherita Corta from Ferrara while the Ceccists as stoutly championed the cause of Francesca della Laguna, surnamed Cecca, from Venice. Mario Chigi, brother of the subsequent Pope Alexander VII, led the former and his more or less serene highness the Prince Aldobrandini the latter. The battle raged furiously and an honorable peace was sought by offering the two ladies rôles of equal importance in Ottavio Tronsarelli's opera "La Catena d'Adone." But the adherents went forward prepared for mighty conflict and an operatic disturbance of the first order was imminent, when the powerful Princess Aldobrandini intervened, forbade both women to sing, and handed over their roles to two evirati.

In these early years of the seventeenth century the opera house was not the only theatre of action for the vocal virtuoso. The church continued to foster musical art, and for a time permitted the voice of woman to be heard within its holy walls. The ancient soloist with his silken robe and flowing locks was succeeded by no less a prima donna than the hitherto secluded nun.

Verovia, of the convent of the Holy Spirit, for several years amazed the world by her vocal feats, while another nun, whose name is lost, but who belonged to Santa Lucia in Selce, was almost equally famous. The cognoscenti of the time deemed these performances by nuns to betoken a noteworthy artistic progress.

The seventeenth century was rich in singers, but for the moment we need note the names of only those who belonged to its earlier years, Nicolini, Biandi, Mario Lorenzino, and Malgigio. Of Vittoria Archilei and Adriana Baroni something has already been said, but we may find a certain piquant interest in the sober assurance of Pietro della Valle that Adriana had in one respect the better of rivalry with Vittoria, in that she was very beautiful, whereas the other was not so at all.

In the social life of Italy these singers were accorded a position worthy of nobles. The most exclusive palaces were opened to them and they mingled with the mighty of the land. Sometimes the lordly patrons made themselves ridiculous, but lordly patrons have done so in all ages. Music came to be regarded as the foremost of the arts to be cultivated in the home. Musical academies, as they were called, were held in many houses, and there are interesting accounts of those held in the residence of Tintoretto in Venice, where his daughter Marietta was the charming hostess. Nothing in the history of this period and the Handelian era so astonishes us as the glory of the male soprano. It seems inconceivable that Caffarelli, Carestini, Farinelli, Senesino, Guadagni (the original Gluck *Orfeo*) and other immortal names were the appellations of men who sang with boys' voices and even sometimes wore petticoats and assumed women's parts. Yet such was the fact and these artificial and unreal singers were the idols of the public.

The history of the operatic male soprano is interesting, if not altogether palatable. His predecessor was the falsettist who imitated the boy soprano by using falsetto tones. Spain produced a line of clever users of the falsetto voice, whose singing early attracted the attention of the authorities of the Roman Church. The Sistine Choir was then reenforced with singers of this type and in recent years, in the course of the reformation of the musical service, the authorities of the Roman Church have restored the use of the falsetto voice.

It was in the fifteenth century that the composers of polyphonic church music found themselves in difficulties by reason of the limited compass of male voices, for at that period women were not employed in choirs. The introduction of falsetto singing enabled the composers to extend their vocal scale to three octaves. Previously it had run about two, ending with the high B of the tenor clef. In the sixteenth century the Spaniards, who apparently had a method unknown to others, ranged through the entire scale of the female soprano. It was the sweetness and pregnant quality of this nondescript voice which made it dear to the church and the falsettist reigned in Rome till the artificial male soprano (the evirato) came to supplant him. Falsettists are still heard in some English and American cathedral choirs, just as they were always heard a quarter of a century ago in the negro minstrel companies in this country.

It is not difficult to account for the great favor which the male soprano enjoyed. The children set apart for vocal careers began their studies very young and mastered the technics of their art at an early age. The artificial voice preserved its purity and elasticity for a long period. It was not uncommon for one of these singers to have a career lasting through forty years. The facility with which their voices executed florid music en-

couraged composers to give them every opportunity to display their skill and these exhibitions
were received with avidity by the public when
the opera became a general entertainment with
the opening of the Teatro San Cassiano in 1637.

When one is studying the score of an early
polyphonic composition he should give close attention to the clefs and the distribution of voices.
The high, or acute, voices were those of boys,
falsettists and evirati. The low or grave were
those of men in the normal scale. The high parts
were entitled "cantus" and "altus" and the lower
ones "tenor" and "bassus."

When the lyric drama began to emerge from
the polyphonic wilderness in which it was quite
lost in the time of Vecchi, the great master of
the madrigal drama (last quarter of the sixteenth
century), the charm of boys' voices and of those
of falsettists and evirati was not put aside. The
title role in Peri's "Daphne" (1597) was sung
by a boy, but that of his "Euridice" (1600) was
allotted to the famous soprano, Vittoria Archilei.

The male soprano did not gain entire supremacy
in the field of the lyric drama in the first years of
the seventeenth century. The distribution of
voices in the various operas shows much uncer-
tainty, but no regard whatever for dramatic fit-

ness, and male sopranos were used quite capriciously.

The title role of Monteverdi's "Orfeo" (1607) was sung by a male soprano. But *Charon* and *Pluto* are basses. When Manelli's "Andromeda" was produced at the opening of the first public opera house, the Teatro San Cassiano, Venice, 1637, the composer sang *Neptune* and his wife *Andromeda*. All the other parts, *Mercury, Perseus, Juno, Venus* and *Astrea*, were sung by men. When Rossi's "Orfeo" was introduced to Paris in 1647 by the Cardinal Mazarin, the shepherd *Aristeus* was sung by the already famous Roman male soprano Marc Antonio Pasqualini. The male soprano held his place even in the early operas of Mozart. In "Mitridate" (1770) and "Lucio Silla" (1772) there were no low voices, and some of the male roles were given to male sopranos.

Before speaking of certain stars of the extinct variety we may ask ourselves again why this sort of singer suddenly became so popular. Those of us who have in recent years heard male sopranos in choirs have perhaps been astonished to find that we were not in the least disturbed by the apparent abnormality. We have listened with pleasure and a vague appreciation of the fitness of the voice to the impersonal character of church music. But without doubt we should be shocked if we heard Julius Caesar, Napoleon or even Romeo singing with a soprano voice. The music lovers of the seventeenth century had no such feeling. The familiarity of musical ears with the voices of boys created a desire to retain as long as possible the juvenile quality of the sound. Even the best and most skilful falsettists could not furnish a perfect replica of this tone. Therefore the method of preservation which seems revolting to us was introduced. The children set apart for vocal careers began their studies very young and at an early age had mastered the technic of their art.

The artificial voice as we have noted preserved its purity and elasticity for a long period. The extended careers of these singers gave them a perennial and inevitable popularity. The facility with which these voices executed florid music induced composers to give them every opportunity for display of their agility, and this continual exhibition of brilliancy was the influence which toward the end of the seventeenth century led to the composition of operas containing only florid roles.

To trace the history of the evirato in detail would be unprofitable, but something may be said about

a few of the great ones. The first artificial male
soprano to be appointed to the Papal Choir was
the Padre Girolamo Rossini, who entered the body
in 1601 and died in 1644. This record defines
the period in which the evirato began his extraordinary career in Italy, whence he was to extend
it over Europe.

Nothing more seems to be known about this
first of all the Rossinis, for once buried in the
retirement of the Papal Chapel he was lost to
history. But those who appeared on the operatic
stage left tangible records behind them. A
descriptive catalogue of these singers would exhibit a striking monotony. It will be more satisfactory to confine our attention to two or three
of the greatest. The first to win fame was Loreto
Vittori, born at Spoleta in 1588. He was attached to the house of Ottavio Doni, father of
the musical historian. He studied under both
Naninis and also Suriano. Afterward he entered
the service of Cosimo de Medici and sang some
of the principal roles in Florentine representations. In these he excited the greatest enthusiasm.
In 1622 he became a singer in the Papal Chapel,
but in spite of this made numerous appearances
in public. He died in 1670, and there is a monu-
ment to him in the Church of Minerva, Rome.

Vittori was a great singer, the greatest master of his time of the young art of operatic recitative created by Peri and Caccini. According to his biographer, Nicias Erythræus, and other contemporaries, this art found its perfect expression in his delivery. It is recorded that his singing moved the public to indescribable transports. Erythræus says that when he sang many persons were almost suffocated with emotion and were obliged hastily to throw open their garments. So great was his popularity in Rome that the people broke into the Palace of the Jesuits at one of his appearances and literally chased out nobles and Cardinals. When people could not get in to his representations they crowded around the palace to try to catch a few echoes through the windows.

To conceive the style of a singer such as this one should study the music of the composers of his time, particularly that of Monteverdi, in some of whose intermezzi Vittori sang at Parma in 1627. One needs also to know something of the way in which the singers of that time were trained. Singing was regarded as part of the education of a gentleman and for fifty years before the beginning of Vittori's public life had been esteemed as one of the noblest arts of Italy.

The famous schools which were formed after the birth of dramatic recitative did not teach the reciters merely to charm the ear, but paid much attention to the appeal to the intelligence. It was deeply felt that the office of the art of recitative was to express justly the sentiment of the poetry. The singer received something of the training of a dramatic poet. At the famous school of Virgilio Mazzochi, one of the celebrated musicians and composers of the time, two hours were devoted every day to the study of letters and the students were taught not only to sing, but to compose. We can readily understand then that the broad, noble, classic declamation of the early period, not unlike the recitative of Gluck's "Orfeo ed Euridice," was delivered by such a master as Vittori in a manner quite justifying the raptures of the hearers, to whom this beautiful art came with the splendor of a revelation.

Vittori was not only a singer but a composer. He wrote several works, of which only his "Galatea" has come down to us. It is a masterpiece of the recitative art. The poem, also by Vittori, is fresh, sweet, natural. It is not unlikely that Handel knew the work well, though no mention is made of it in Sedley Taylor's book on Handel's indebtedness to other composers. But this absorbing figure in the early history of singing must be set aside, or passing mention may extend itself easily to a chapter.

A younger contemporary of Vittori was the celebrated Baldassare Ferri, born at Perugia, December 6, 1610. He became a chorister at Orvieto in 1621. In 1625 a Polish prince carried him off to his father's court, whence in 1665 he was transferred to Germany, and finally returned to die in Italy in 1680. Enthusiasm followed him everywhere. Sonnets by the hundred were written about him. People covered his carriage with flowers if he sang but a single song. He was a handsome man, with a beautiful soprano voice, marvellous in its liquid translucence and its flexibility. Bontempi, the historian of music, wrote of him:

"One who has not heard this sublime singer can form no idea of the limpidity of his voice, of his agility, of his marvellous facility in the execution of the most difficult passages, of the justness of his intonation, the brilliancy of his trill, of his inexhaustible respiration. One often heard him perform rapid and difficult passages with every shade of crescendo and diminuendo. Then, when it seemed as if he ought to be tired, he would launch into his interminable trill and mount and descend on it all the degrees of the chromatic scale through a range of two octaves with unerring justice. And all this was but play for him, so that the muscles of his face did not indicate the least effort. Moreover, gifted with sentiment and imagination, he imparted to all this singing a touching expression."

Truly the colorature singing of the evirati was something worth hearing. Here we may with propriety overstep our chronological limits in order to gain enlightenment from a moment's view of a later period.

All the histories are prolific in stories of the vocal art of Caffarelli and Farinelli, the two greatest male sopranos who sang in the Handelian period. But it seems better in continuing this retrospect of the vocal past to revive memories of singers of whom less is usually written. Carestini's splendid art saved the day for Handel when Farinelli was singing at the opposition theatre in 1733. The composer had not been able to get him in the previous season because he was engaged in Milan. Handel took Senesino instead and this singer created a furor in London. But Carestini was probably a greater artist. One learns what singers received in those times from a letter written to Mr. Walpole by Owen Swiny. He quotes

1,200 guineas as the price to be offered for either Carestini or Senesino. This of course was for the season.

Carestini was born in Ancona in 1705 (or thereabout) and lived till about 1760. His debut was made at Rome in 1721 in a female role, that of *Costanza* in Boncini's "Griselda." Carestini began life as a soprano, but his voice changed to contralto, and it was this which brought him into comparison with Senesino, also a contralto. It is not altogether clear what his contemporaries mean when they speak of his voice, because one tells us that it was one of the deepest and richest contraltos ever heard, while Quantz, the distinguished flutist, records its range as from D to G. In 1723 Carestini sang in Prague at the coronation of Charles VI. Turning to the pages of Burney's "Present State of Music in Germany" we find this sentence:

"When he performed in Prague his compass was sixteen notes from B in the bass to C in alt."

One thing alone remains quite certain, namely, that he was a contralto and that he sang admirably. The question of the range of voice among the evirati is one that need not give any student serious trouble. The composers of the time wrote for the singers, and therefore their scores furnish presumptive evidence as to the range of the voices. No extremely high notes appear in these old scores. In a brilliant cadenza sung by Farinelli and reproduced in Mr. Krehbiel's "Music and Manners" the highest note is the upper A. The lowest is E. But in an air from Hasse's "Artaserse" sung by Farinelli we find low B. A cadenza written by Hasse for the famous female contralto Vittoria Tesi runs only from D to E, an octave and one tone. We owe the preservation of these records to the taste of the English poet Thomas Gray, who made an invaluable collection of airs of his time. This collection is now in the possession of Mr. H. E. Krehbiel.

To return to Carestini, we find all authorities agreeing that he sang rapid passages with remarkable skill, and that in later life he greatly improved his cantilena. A man of excellent appearance, he made a careful study of stage action, and was a master of the pantomimic art. His vocal study was unceasing. Mancini says:

"Although his voice was naturally beautiful he did not neglect to perfèct it by study and to make it suitable to every kind of song, and he raised it to a point so sublime that he established in his youth his fame. He had a fecund genius and a discernment so delicate that despite the excellence of everything he did his great modesty prevented him from being satisfied. One day one of his friends finding him at study and applauding his singing, he turned to him and said: 'My friend, if I do not succeed in satisfying myself, how can I satisfy others?' "

Mancini, it should be noted, heard most of the singers of whom he writes and was qualified to pronounce opinions of them. He was a vocal teacher, was born in 1716, died in 1800, and published his book "Practical Reflections on Florid Song" in 1796. This book is the chief authority on the singers and singing of the time. It has been translated into English. Francesco Tosi's book on florid song was published much earlier than Mancini's and contains, alas! no sketches of singers. It also omits things about vocal art which many of us would like very much to know.

It would not be especially profitable to recount in detail the lives of such artists as Grossi, Orsini, Velluti and others. Their careers were much alike, and their art was of one general type. Wherever we read in the works of those who heard these famous vocal artists of early times, whether it be in the records of professional musicians like Quantz, historians of high musical education like Burney, or cultivated amateurs like Lord Mount Edgecumb, we get the same idea of their singing. These male sopranos and contraltos all sang with exquisite technical finish, with thoroughly equalized scales, with suavity and elegance.

The admirable Dr. Burney wrote an essay on criticism, and conveniently introduced it into the third volume of his compendious history. This essay throws much light on the musical performances of its day by telling us what was expected. In regard to opera and operatic singing the author says:

"In hearing dramatic music little attention is pointed by the audience to anything but the airs and powers of the principal singers, and yet if the character, passion and importance of each personage in the piece is not distinctly marked and supported, if the airs are not contrasted with one another and the part of every singer in the same scene specially different in measure, compass, time and style, the composer is not a complete master of his profession.

"Good singing requires a clear, sweet, even and flexible voice, equally free from nasal and guttural defects. It is but by the tone of voice and articulation of words that a vocal performer is superior to an instrumental. If in swelling a note the voice trembles and varies in pitch, or the intonations are false, ignorance and science are equally offended; and if a perfect shake, good taste in embellishment and a touching expression be wanting, the singer's reputation will make no great progress among true judges. If in rapid divisions the passages are not executed with neatness and articulation, or in adagios if light and shade, pathos, variety of coloring and expression are wanting the singer may have merit of certain kinds, but is still distant from perfection."

One of the items in this enumeration is "divisions," another name for "diminutions." Burney tells us that these divisions were to be sung with neatness and articulation. In other words, they were to be perfectly clean cut and absolutely smooth. There was no call for power or brilliancy. Exactness and elegance were demanded, but not that sweeping manner which much later entered operatic music in the true dramatic bravura of Mozart.

We note that Burney also speaks of "swelling a note." The place of this "messa di voce" in seventeenth century art has already been shown. Upon a command of it rest to-day all the infinitesimal gradations of loudness and softness which play such an important part in the nuancing of song. In the Handelian period certain arias were introduced into operas chiefly for the sake of giving singers opportunity to display their skill in this technical feat. These were called arias di portamento and they were slow movements in which the voice slid languorously from one tone to another and lingered with a swell on each important note. Such airs were suited only to sentimental scenes or to moments in which tearful melancholy was to be expressed.

Taste in embellishment is also mentioned by Burney. Singers of Handel's time, like their predecessors, were permitted wide latitude in the matter of adding ornaments to their numbers. But we must bear in mind that the eighteenth century singers were as a rule soundly trained in music and knew how to make their embellishments. Here again the experience of their auditors exercised a wholesome restraint upon them for pretty nearly every operagoer knew what was permissible and what was not.

In fine, a word may be said about the "touching expression" required by Burney. We read over and over of the wonderful effect of the singing of these ancients upon their hearers.

People were deeply, even violently, moved by them. When, however, we come to examine closely the comments of contemporaries upon the traits of their art and to refer to the scores of the operas in which they sang we are brought to the conclusion that their loftiest flights of expression, precisely like those of Vittori and Ferri, were in the domain of tender pathos.

Burney must be read literally. "Touching expression," "pathos," these were the features of the eloquence of the Farinellis and Carestinis. There is nothing in the writing of those who heard them nor in the scores of the operas themselves to indicate that any approach toward the publication of tumultuous elemental passion was even attempted. Surely we may conclude that with the first entry of this fundamental element of tragedy into the Italian opera the male sopranos and contraltos were doomed. Their existence was prolonged by a distorted state of public taste which regarded the opera as a field for the display of vocal technic and voices entirely sweet and gentle. When dramatic verity claimed recognition the incongruous mixture of high voices had to give way to a normal distribution in which masculine and feminine qualities played their appropriate parts.

CHAPTER XI

THE SEVENTEENTH CENTURY ITALIAN OPERA

WITHOUT question the seventeenth century was the most important in the early history of opera. For that reason its relation to the art of singing possessed a significance not to be over-looked. The century began with a genuine lyric drama; it ended with a superficial spectacular opera. It began with vocal ideals founded on pure classic beauty; it closed with singing which might well be called baroque at its worst. Its first years saw the musical drama cherished as a lofty art by a limited but cultivated society of intellectuals; its decline beheld that same form degraded to the level of a mere show for the entertainment of an amusement loving multitude. It opened with the composer exercising freely the divine prerogatives of creative genius; it finished with the singer deified by the populace and the composer relegated to the service of fashioning the crown of laurels for his lofty brow.

The fine musical perceptions of Monteverdi

made little impression on his immediate successors. It will be recalled by students of musical history that this great master left us at least one specimen of the aria form in its embryonic state, namely "Lasciatemi morire" from the opera "Arianna," that exquisite fragment of which Marco da Gagliano, a contemporary composer, said, "It visibly moved the entire theatre to tears." The chaste simplicity and eloquent expressiveness of such music was appreciated only by the elect. Nor did the cognoscenti recognize the significance of the master's innovations in harmony. Monteverdi's supreme musical achievement was the discovery of the use of the dissonance in the expression of dramatic passion. He was the sire of the whole race of impressionists, modernists, futurists (call them what you will); for he liberated musical art from the monastic reticence of churchly polyphony; and while his influence led to the defilement of the crystal fountains of Lasso and Palestrina, it opened the way for the outpour of those torrents of musical utterance that thunder through the scores of Wagner.

Never a purist, as purism was understood in his day, he marched further and further from the sculpturesque elegance of the Hellenic style till in the final years of his Venetian period we find him producing the pompous pages of his spectacular "L'Incoronazione di Poppea." From 1616 he had truthfully written his signature "Claudio Monteverdi, Veniziano," and from 1639, with his "L'Adone" composed for the new Teatro San Cassiano, he had indissolubly united himself with the young army of seekers after public applause. In the years between the revelation of Monteverdi's "Orfeo" and the presentation of his "L'Adone" the youthful Italian opera underwent a remarkable transformation. Nor was the movement in any manner impeded by the appearance of the clearly defined vocal forms of Francesco Cavalli.

The solo "Delizie contente" in his "Giasone" (1649) is a well-shaped aria da capo, and from it undoubtedly descended the long line of airs of the Handelian era. Yet the fact confronts us that the majority of the opera composers of the early seventeenth century were writers of elaborate and often ornate recitatives. In this they merely followed the fashions of the ecclesiastic music of their day. One finds a striking similarity in construction between the psalms of Severi (1616) and the recitatives of Stefano Landi's "San Alessio" (1634). "La Catena d'Adone" by Domenico Mazzochi (1626), "Diana

Schernita" by Emilio Cornachi (1629) "Erminia
sul Giordano" by Michaelangelo Rossi (1637)
and others. Those who wish to examine this
music will find whole scenes quoted in that excellent work "Studien zur Geschichte der Italien-
ischen Oper im 17. Jahrhundert" by Hugo Goldschmidt.

It is not essential to the present work that
quotations should be made from these scores. The
point to be observed is that within a few years
the obliteration of the pure lines of the young
stile parlante by the florid decorations of vocal
ornament had made astonishing advances and the
virtuoso had assumed a prominence which even
the supreme singers of the first operas sacrificed
to the noble simplicity of the ensemble.

The cultivation of the cantata was a powerful
factor in the development of the public taste in
song in the seventeenth century. The "cantata
da camera" supplied to the homes of the cultured
in seventeenth century Italy what the art song
gives to those of to-day. It owed its existence
to the popularity of the newly invented recitative,
and indeed in the beginning was merely a short
dramatic narrative told in recitative by a single
voice. In time the aria was introduced and by
degrees the form became more elaborate. The

concert arias of the classic period, such as Mendelssohn's "Infelice" and Beethoven's "Ah, perfido," were the lineal descendants of the cantata. The greatest master of the cantata form in the seventeenth century was Giovanni Carissimi (1604?-1674). Alessandro Scarlatti, who was probably a pupil of Carissimi in the latter's old age, was also a prolific writer of cantatas. His earliest, such as "Il Germanico" and "Il Corilano," were often, as his biographer E. J. Dent notes, "little more than lectures on Roman history, set to recitative with an occasional aria." Doubtless the popularity of the cantata in the first years of the century was due to the fact that lyric music had not yet come into the presence of the general public. It was a pleasure of cultivated society. The people knew little of musical art, but the works of the distinguished composers were cherished in the palaces and were preserved for us in the libraries of nobles or churches. That they were not widely disseminated is proved by the fact that more than one manuscript copy of a work is seldom found. We must remember that the technic of vocal art was far in advance of that of instruments and the only virtuoso known to the amateurs of the time was the singer. Consequently he was expected to exhibit all his powers and to embellish the cantata with ornaments of his own. It is improbable that the audiences of that period often heard airs sung as they come down to us in the manuscript.

In these first years of the seventeenth century the entire apparatus of the opera slowly developed itself and its various functions separated themselves and acquired the well demarked relationships essential to an organized art form. Musical figure, as outlined by Monteverdi, advanced to the foreground in the works of such writers as Cavalli, and its purpose was clearly differentiated from that of recitative. The orchestra gradually assumed shape and gained interest, while the infant breathings of instrumental music offered suggestions to writers for the voice.

With astonishing rapidity the opera developed into a mere amusement. The more easily grasped features of it, to wit, the arias and the florid singing, became the centers of public attention, and the accomplishments of the singers rose daily to higher consideration. The apparatus of the opera indeed took an almost geometrical clearness of shape and equally an almost geometrical conventionality. As an art form it fell with the swiftness of a shooting star from the place which as a product of feeble and dying Hellenism it had sought to occupy in Italy. It was while Monteverdi was still active in the world of music that the influence of Venice began, as we have intimated, to make itself felt in the development of opera, and the opening of the Teatro San Cassiano in 1637, which has already been mentioned, marked the beginning of a century of efflorescent style. The opening of the theatre gave opera to the general public, and the character of that public is admirably suggested in the impassioned words in which Symonds in his "Renaissance in Italy" describes Venice.

"Free, isolated, wealthy, powerful; famous throughout Europe for the pomp of her state equipage and for the immorality of her private manners; ruled by a prudent aristocracy, who spent vast wealth on public shows and on the maintenance of a more than imperial civic majesty; Venice, with her pavements of liquid chrysoprase, with her palaces of porphyry and marble, her frescoed façades, her quays and squares aglow with the costumes of the Levant, her lagoons afloat with the galleys of all nations, her churches floored with mosaics, her silvery domes and ceilings glittering with sculptures bathed in molten gold; Venice, luxurious in the light and color of her atmosphere, where sea

mists rose into the mounded summer clouds;
arched over by the broad expanse of sky, bounded
only by the horizon of waves and plain and distant mountain ranges, and reflected in all of its
many hues of sunrise and sunset upon the glassy
surface of smooth waters; Venice, asleep like a
miracle of opal or pearl upon the bosom of an
undulating lake—here and here only on the face
of the whole globe was the unique city wherein
the pride of life might combine with the lustre
of the physical universe to create and stimulate
in the artist a sense of all that was most sump-
tuous in the pageant of the world of sense."

This was the Venice of the sixteenth century,
the Venice of Titian, Tintoretto and Veronese.
If the middle of the seventeenth century saw this
proud state stripped of something of its ancient
power, it found her still masterful enough to hold
absolute dominion over the Adriatic, to defy the
anathema of Rome, and to conquer the brilliant
arms of the aggressive Turk. Venice was still
rich, self centered, luxurious, sensual and independent. To her appetite for spectacle the bud-
ding opera appealed with all the seductions of an
art addressed to at least two of her greedy senses.
And her mood was prepared for the new strains
of the regenerated lyric play. She, too, had been

wearied by the performance of tragedies set to funeral music; and the opera, with its rapidly developing riches, its gorgeous stage trappings, and its growing display of the dazzling feats of the voice, opened to her a new world of artistic form and color.

The opera with which the Teatro San Cassiano was opened in 1637 was "Andromeda," book by Benedetto Ferrari, music by Francesco Manelli. The same writers supplied the novelty for the next season and in 1639 was produced "Le Nozze di Tito e Peleo," book by Oratio Persiani, music by Francesco Cavalli. For many seasons thereafter Cavalli was the favorite composer for this theatre. One now unknown work of Monteverdi, "Il Ritorno d'Ulisse in Patria," was given in 1641, and his "Arianna" was heard at the Teatro San Moisé when that house was opened in 1639. But Galvani's admirable history of the Venetian theatre of the seventeenth century does not contain any mention of a performance of his "Orfeo." Such a work would surely have been too chaste for the seventeenth century Venetians.

In what manner the opera seized their fancy may be gathered from the speed with which lyric theatres were built. Besides the operatic theatres already mentioned the following were opened in Venice in the seventeenth century: San Giovanni e Paolo, 1639; Novissimo, 1641; Ss. Apostoli, 1649, St. Apollinare, 1651; San Salvatore, 1661; Ai Saloni, 1670; San Angelo, 1677; San Giovanni Grisostomo, 1678; Canal Reggio, 1679; Alla Zattere, 1679; Altieri, 1690; Santa Marina, 1698; San Fantino, 1699; and San Moisé (private), 1699.

The Doric nobility of the classic Monteverdi style abandoned, the opera transformed by the genius of Cavalli into a slender stem of recitative bearing luxurious blossoms of aria, and the singer raised to the imperial purple in the domain of operatic art, the state of the lyric drama in the Venetian republic and throughout Italy near the close of the seventeenth century may easily be realized.

Reverting to the "San Alessio" of Stephano Landi (1634), we find all the voices used with equal brilliancy. The recitatives retain something of the ecclesiastical style. Many of them have prolonged grupetti on the final cadences, and some have repeats, like couplets, followed by orchestral ritornelli. The airs are generally short, of one movement, and with some ornaments. The composer evidently sought for expression rather than empty decoration. One air for San Alessio in the second act is especially admirable. The duets and trios are numerous and nearly all show insight and interpretative ability. According to the fashion of the time which called for "comic relief" there are two comic duos. From this element of the serious opera the opera buffa developed, as the historians have clearly shown. Landi wrote skilfully for the voice, but he must have had a bass of extraordinary equipment for the role of the demon, which extends from C below the F clef to the F above it. The choruses are written in madrigal style in six, eight and even more parts.

But choruses dwindled in opera scores as the century advanced, and in the final years the rule was to have only one, and that to finish the work. High voices gradually assumed the supremacy which they retained in Handel's day and the opera became a vocal concerto. The style of the latter years of the seventeenth century is exemplified in such a work as "Il Cariere de se Medesima" by Alessandro Melani (1681). The music is very light and florid. The bass sings numerous and long roulades. The song of April for soprano in Act 2 is a bewildering display of rapid ascending and descending passages, vocalises, trills, staccati and holds. The role of Roberto must have been written for a soprano with a voice extremely light and flexible. It is the chief part, but the others are by no means unimportant and all are florid.

At the close of the seventeenth century the opera differed little in construction from the cantata with its long duets, arias and final chorus. The voices were principally soprano and alto (male and female) and a few tenors. The bass fell more and more into disuse except in operas of buffa or demi-caratere type. Music had ceded her position to the virtuoso. It may be interesting to note in passing that in the score of "Cesare in Alessandria" by Aldo Vrandini (Naples, 1700) the influence of Corelli's violin school appears, and there is a remarkably fine obbligato to a soprano solo.

After a survey of the works of his immediate predecessors one is not astonished at some of the productions of Alessandro Scarlatti, who began his artistic career when opera was in the state just described. In his "Le Nezze col Nemico" is an aria called the "Canto di Rossignuolo." In it the composer assembled all the accomplishments of the art of singing. The soloist was accompanied by one lute and one violin in order that the voice might be left in high relief according to the style of the time. The orchestra was heard only in the ritornello. All the known ornaments and vocalises were introduced in this astonishing air, among them a chain of trills mounting without pause from F to F of the treble clef.

The correspondent of the *Mercure de France* resident in Venice in the last years of the seventeenth century was much interested in opera. His letters convince us that toward 1700 the Italian musical stage concerned itself less and less with lyric drama, and the singer's only competitor was the scene painter. At the beginning of the eighteenth century all this apparel, decorative and instrumental, was stripped from the opera in order to leave the vocal virtuoso facing his public with nothing save his art and the suppleness of his voice. In commenting on the paucity of choruses the writer says that the Venetians do not need them since they enjoy so much elaborate polyphonic church music with instrumental accompaniment (theorbos, viols, little organs and clavecins).

"Singers," he says, "are called virtuosi. The Italians dearly love high voices and have not so much taste for basses." The Venetians, like the impresarios of to-day, scoured Europe for the best voices and paid fabulous prices.

"The voices," declares this observant reporter, "are clear, pure, solid and bold, without pinching or constraint. The women understand music to perfection, manage their voices admirably, and have a certain manner of trills, cadences and echoes, which they vary and conduct as they please."

After a grand aria the audience would shout "Viva bella! Viva ah cara! Sia benedetta." And when the singers left the theatre the gondoliers would with equal fervor call down blessings on their glorified heads.

CHAPTER XII

DISTRIBUTION OF VOICES IN OPERA

SOME insight into the manner of distributing voices in musical compositions has already been obtained by the reader. But a closer scrutiny of this matter is now practicable. The selection of voices for the interpretation of roles in dramatic works appears to have been governed at times by caprice and at other times by a feeling for propriety. But at whatever period we examine the use of voices we shall find that public taste had a certain amount of influence and that in the seventeenth century it operated entirely to the deterioration of dramatic art.

The musical drama began with a normal employment of voices. Men sang male characters and with masculine voices. If women did not always impersonate women, at least boys did. Later we find abnormality triumphant. The public, having lost all appreciation of dramatic verity and regarding opera as a mere field for the exhibition of vocal accomplishments, cared nothing at all about the timbre of a voice so long as it was beautiful and skilfully used.

We should undoubtedly be amazed to find Julius Caesar singing soprano or Achilles contralto, but the opera goers of the late seventeenth century and those of the "golden age of bel canto" would have been very much astonished if either of them had been a baritone or a bass. At most they could have been tenors, but neither in that case would have been the principal personage in the drama. He would have surely been a soprano.

It is impossible to trace step by step the change from the normal to the abnormal because we have not sufficiently full records of the casts of the earliest works. It is safe to say that voices were rationally employed in Poliziano's "Orfeo" (1472). The male soprano had not risen to fame in Italy at that time. Baccio Ugolino, who sang the title role, was a "cantore a liuto" and may have been either a tenor or a baritone. Who sang the other parts we do not know. But there is no reason for supposing that they were entrusted to voices unsuited to the characters.

The few musical examples which have come down to us from the various intermezzi and spectacular musical plays of the sixteenth century show that the composers treated the voices largely according to the circumstances of each occasion, but with a harmonic plan similar to that of modern part writing. Sopranos sang women's roles when there were any. If not, the principal lyric voice was the tenor. In the madrigal dramas of Orazzio Vecchi and his pupil Banchieri we find that female voices represent the utterance of female characters and male voices that of men. When the Florentines invented recitative and began to write their lyric dramas in the new style, they followed Vecchi in the use of the normal quality of voices. They caused men to sing men's roles and women those of women. The progress of vocal part writing had been steadily toward the domination of high voices in the harmonic structure, and with these adventurous young composers there was no thought of depriving soprano and tenor of their commanding positions. But aside from the purely harmonic reason there was the dramatic. The Florentine innovators were not trying to focus the attention of the cognoscenti on music planned to exhibit the resources of the human voice, but to place before the cultivated hearers a lyric drama in which the emotion, the situation or the scene, was the dominating factor, and the medium of communication a fluid transparent musical speech of which the most striking modern counterpart is the dialogue of Debussy's "Pelleas et Melisande."

Whether the singers of the first Italian operas employed in their performances any of that marvellous skill in ornamentation which they possessed in such a high degree we can only conjecture. The probabilities are strongly against the presumption that they did, because the writings of the composers should satisfy us that anything in the shape of florid disguise of their simple textual declamations would have been entirely foreign to their purposes.

In Peri's "Euridice" (1600) the composer, himself a tenor, sang the Orfeo and the title role was confided to the celebrated Vittoria Archilei, the foremost soprano of the hour. We can usually learn how these early composers distributed their voices by the simple process of observing what clefs they used. They did not confine themselves to treble and bass clefs, as our modern writers do, but habitually employed the soprano, alto and tenor, in addition to the bass. Sometimes the clef is misleading as in the case of Monteverdi's "Orfeo." The title role is written on the tenor clef and was undoubtedly intended to be sung by a tenor, but the original of the part was a male soprano. Euridice and Proserpina were written on the soprano clef, Pluto and Charon on the bass. Pluto in all his manifestations has been a bass ever since.

When the male soprano entered the field his position was not uncontested. We read of several famous tenors in the early years of the seventeenth century. But the male soprano slowly encroached upon their territory and in the end wholly displaced them. The ascent of the male soprano to the supreme position we must attribute not only to the general decadence of Italian taste in the period of her literary and artistic decline, but to the fact that the trend of this taste was in the direction of admiration for ornament. The literary phrase maker and the baroque architect were the creators of artistic products fundamentally akin to the luxurious vocal style which slowly superseded the noble recitative of the Florentines and to which the fluid and voluptuous male soprano voices lent themselves with such signal success.

The result, as we have seen, was the rapid development of a public demand for exhibitions of all the powers of singing voices and a speedy extinction of appreciation of the dramatic possibilities of the opera. The first works of the Italian composers for the lyric stage possessed a dignity and sincerity which have never been surpassed in the theatre. Yet in less than forty years almost every vestige of dramatic verity was obliterated and the opera transformed into a field for the display of vocal technic. The rise of the male soprano voice to supremacy was a part of the whole change, and in the astonishing distribution of voices in the operas we find a demonstration of the complete indifference of the public to anything resembling dramatic illusion.

When the Teatro San Cassiano, the first public opera house, was opened in Venice in 1637, the first opera to be produced was "Andromeda," the book by Benedetto Ferrari and the music by Francesco Manelli. The composer sang the role of Neptune, and his wife, Maddalena Manelli, was the Andromeda. All the other parts, including Mercury, Perseus, Juno, Venus and Astrea, were allotted to men. This convinces us that already the male soprano and contralto were in the full blaze of their glory. In 1647 Cardinal Mazarin carried a whole company of Italian singers from Rome to Paris and introduced the Italian opera to the French with a performance of Luigi Rossi's "Orfeo." Atto Melani, a tenor with a voice of moderate range, sang the title role. A soprano known as La Checca was the Euridice. The shepherd, Aristeus, was sung by the famous male soprano, Marc Antonio Pasqualini. Rosina Martini was the Venus, and a male soprano, whose name has not come down to us, was the Nurse. How swiftly the new order of things came into domination may be guessed from the casts of two operas by Stefano Landi. His work on the standard mythological theme and entitled "La Morte d'Orfeo" was produced in Venice in 1619. Orfeo was a tenor; Euridice a female soprano; Thetis, soprano; Calliope, mother of Orfeo, soprano; Philenus, tenor; Charon, bass. All the men were represented by men, all the women by women. In the same musician's "San Alessio," produced at Rome in 1634, we find the roles distributed thus: San Alessio, male soprano; Martin and Curtio, two pages, sopranos; Madre, female soprano; Sposa, female soprano; Demonio, bass.

It would not profit to follow the catalogue of operas to the end of the century. The employment of the male soprano continued, as all students of musical history know, till the beginning of the nineteenth century. The famous interpreters of Scarlatti's heroic roles and the impersonators of Handel's warriors and demi gods were men who sang with the voices of women.

At the beginning of the career of Mozart we find the Italian opera still dominated by the artificial voice. The distribution of the parts in Mozart's "Mitridate," produced in 1770, was as follows: Mitridate, tenor; Aspasia, soprano, Siface, male soprano; Farnace, contralto; Ismene, second soprano and Arbate, soprano. There was not a low voice in the score. A similar arrangement is found in "Lucio Silla," written in 1772; Lucio Silla, tenor; Giunia, soprano; Cecilio, a senator, male soprano; Lucio Sinna (a man), female soprano; Celia, soprano, and Aufidio, tenor.

Closer adherence to truth was revealed in Mozart's arrangement of the roles in "Le Nozze di Figaro" and "Don Giovanni." Both works followed the lead of the Italian opera buffa which had long dissociated itself from the opera seria in the allotment of voices. The opera buffa depended for its interest largely upon the delineation of character, the movement of intrigue and the vivacity of its action. The public attention was not wholly centred upon the achievements of the vocal virtuosi. Mozart, whose artistic instincts were exquisitely sensitive, felt the need of character portrayal more keenly than any of his contemporaries; and to his fine perceptions in this department of his art we owe the inexhaustible vitality of his masterpieces. We must not forget that he himself described "Don Giovanni" as an opera buffa, while "Die Zauberflöte" was a true German singspiel. In his work, as in the other two, we find the voices normally employed. The protagonists are tenor and soprano, while the colorature soprano and the bass are accessories to the action just as surely as they are in "Les Huguenots" of many years later.

The immense popularity of the opera buffa may be seen in the list of productions in a single theatre in the latter part of the eighteenth century. At La Scala from 1784 to 1789 inclusive there were 46 productions of which 27 were opera buffa works and two were farces. Although the employment of the singing voice in the opera buffa yielded little to the artificialities of the pompous opera seria, it could not entirely escape its influence. The supremacy of the high voice was for a time almost as clear in the comic as in the tragic opera. A typical score of the middle of the seventeenth century, for example, is that of "Dai Male il Bene," text by Cardinal Rispigliosi, music by Maria Abbatini and Marco Marazzoli, produced at the marriage of the Prince of

Palestrina and Olimpia Giustiniani in 1654. Here we find that the characters are Leonora and Marina, sopranos; Fernando and Diego, tenors, and Tabacco, a baritone or high bass, probably of the buffo type.

In the time of Alessandro Scarlatti it was customary to employ in almost every serious opera what the modern dramatists call the "comic relief." This led to one singular selection of voices. The comedians were usually an old woman and an old man. The former was almost invariably impersonated by a tenor, and this despite the fact that in the same opera the tragic female parts might be sung by artificial male sopranos. The comic old woman's companion, the comic old man, was a buffo basso. In the development of this character arose the time honored custom of the Italian buffos of frequently breaking into the falsetto. It was originally the pipe and whistle of the old man.

It is not essential to give further details about the use of voices in the Scarlatti period, since all students of musical history know that the reign of the male soprano was in its glory still later in the days of Handel. In the Handelian era it was almost the first law of opera that the principal male singer (primo uomo) should be a soprano. The secondo uomo or second male singer was either a soprano or a contralto and the third a tenor. When a fourth male character was introduced he was usually a bass. Three women's roles were the required number and the prima donna was always a high soprano. Sometimes as in "Teseo" (London, 1723) all the male parts were in the hands of artificial sopranos and contraltos and they had all the important arias. During the entire performance of such an opera not one masculine note was heard.

It is impossible to determine the moment at which the transition was made to the modern custom of distributing voices in opera. Plainly enough the present method was not new; it was older than that of Scarlatti and Handel for Peri and Caccini used it. The modern masters merely returned to the method which respected dramatic verity. At La Scala, for example, we find Veluti, the last of the great male sopranos, singing the principal role in Rossini's "Aureliano in Palmira" when that work was produced in 1814. In 1817 the records show Donzelli, the famous tenor, singing the chief male roles in Paer's "Achille," De Winter's "Maometta" and Generali's "Roderigo di Valenzo." In 1818 the tenor was the distinguished Giovanni David. and in 1819 and 1820 the great Crivelli, one of the master tenors of history, was at the head of nearly every cast.

Possibly the return of the tenor to his leading position in opera may have been influenced by the advent of the famous Anton Raff, who made his debut in Florence in 1738 and later sang in Naples under the management of Farinelli. Mozart wrote the part of Idomeneo for him. However, the one clear fact seems to be that for some time in the course of the latter half of the eighteenth century there was no established practice. The virtuoso, as the brilliant singer of florid music was called, was generally a male soprano and for him the composers wrote their leading roles; but when an accomplished tenor was available, he was utilized. When Veluti made his first appearance in London in 1825, there was already evidence of public distaste for the male soprano voice.

Five years later Bellini's "Il Pirata" was produced and the chief singers were Donzelli, Malibran and Lablache. In the following year (1831) "La Sonnambula" and "Anna Bolena" were brought forward and the foremost members of the company were Pasta, Rubini, Edward Seguin and Lablache. The male soprano had taken his farewell of the London stage. He had already disappeared from La Scala. The distribution of voices in opera was no longer determined by the necessity of providing the artificially prepared virtuoso with music suited to a brilliant display of his powers. A reaction had set in and the trend was toward dramatic characterization. Without doubt the romantic movement gave the opera an impulse in the new direction, but we cannot discuss this topic here. The custom became established of giving the role of the hero to a tenor, that of the heroine to a soprano, while the darker voices of the contralto and the baritone were habitually employed to utter the sentiments of the unfortunate or wicked personages in the story.

CHAPTER XIII

EARLY IDEALS OF SINGING

THE limits of this work have necessarily been overstepped in some places, yet the temptation to enter upon a comparison of old and new ideals of singing need not be resisted. The student of vocal history may easily trace the development of the modern style by observing at what period in the march of operatic composition the orchestra began to rival the voice as an instrument of expression and by noting when the conventionalism of the familiar classic subjects began to give way to the passionate and even violent tales of the romanticists. He may trace, if he will, the influence of Victor Hugo and Byron on the lyric drama, and he may with profit study the histories of such singers as Pasta, Malibran, Rubini, and others of the world famous group whose art glorified the Theatre des Italiens in the early years of the nineteenth century.

If he examines the pages of the old composers, he will seek in vain for such a num-

ber as "Di quella pira," that time honored
triumph of tenors in Verdi's "Il Trovatore." The
exclamatory violence of this music, its shrieking
climax in the high C, and its proclamation of
an emotion tumultuous and tragic are all foreign
to the style which dominated operatic art, and
consequently all singing, up to the time of Gluck
and Mozart.

With all their genius in expression, their new
and admirable use of instruments as means of
dramatic expression, their fidelity to the purposes
of the poets whose texts they set, and above all
their consummate mastery of the art of dramatic
declamation, these two masters were in style the
logical products of a century and a half of
development, of which the first impulses originated in the ecclesiastical chant.

When the modern romantic movement began,
the manner of Mozart and that of Gluck underwent a subtle, but significant alteration. Gluck
had voiced dramatic feeling in sweeping and magnificent melodic utterances, such as "Divinités du
Styx." Mozart had lifted the ancient recitative
to the grandiose level of his orchestrated declamation in such imposing scenes as that of Donna
Anna beginning, "Don Ottavio, son morta." He
had also demonstrated that the ancient coloratura

could be made to serve purely dramatic purposes. The Queen of the Night singing "Gli angui d'inferno" and the Donnas in "Don Giovanni" publishing their emotions in elaborate roulades brought the florid style to its loftiest development.

When Weber wrote "Der Freischütz" and "Euryanthe," he made a step forward toward the modern dramatic form. He united cantilena of almost a folk song character with declamatory recitative as broad as Mozart's and with a splendid bravura as delineative as it was brilliant. In "Ocean, thou mighty monster" we have the supreme example of this new form, to which none of the ancient titles will apply. It has therefore been called the "scena dramatica" or dramatic scene. Beethoven adopted it when he composed the great "Abscheulicher" in "Fidelio." And finally Wagner based his endless melody on it as surely as if he had intentionally sat before the scores of his adored Weber to steal their honey.

The old masters approached their art from a different angle, and the old singers were required to accomplish their artistic purposes in ways simpler and chaster than those open to the modern declaimer. The characteristic style of the sixteenth century was contrapuntal music into which the singers, as we have seen, scattered those variegated flowers of song which had been their chief delight in the era of improvised descant. This polyphonic music was written by all the great masters of the period and in this style we find most of the first attempts at lyric drama which led to modern opera. The introduction of the monodic song began a great new epoch. With this introduction disappeared the primitive vocal art of the middle ages, an art nevertheless difficult and demanding of the singers a serious knowledge of music and a solid vocal technic.

When the singers entered the new field of activity provided by the opera, they carried with them their pure elegant cantilena, which was the basis of church music singing, together with their skill in ornaments and their ability to improvise the long flourishes of their scroll work cadenzas, such as they had used for their alleluias. The most cursory examination of the recitatives of the earliest operas and the ecclesiastic music of the same period, such as the "Salmi Passaggiati" of Severi, will serve to satisfy the student that there was absolutely no technical difference between the two styles of composition. Consequently there was no need of any addition to the established technic and style of singing. Any church singer could sing the opera music of his time. The only novelty he would confront would be found in the nature of the text and the emergence of human expression.

We see the florid element of vocal art speedily finding its way into the dramatic music and finally coming to be the general delight of audiences when opera became a public amusement. At the same time the smooth and elegant delivery of cantilena retained its place in the system. In short, the cantabile with all that its name implies in sustained equality, smoothness and beauty of tone, in finish of phrasing and delicacy of accent, was one factor of the vocal art of this time, while the other was floridity with all that its name implies in the way of clarity, equality, undulatory grace and airy suspension. That these two elements were distinctly marked in the contrapuntal music of the sixteenth century is clearly shown in any performance of the works of the masters by such organizations as the Musical Art Society.

When the monody was introduced, these elements were transferred to music for the solo voice and became the means of expression known to the first opera composers. The expressive power of this music has been underrated. It is underrated to-day because when it is heard it is heard inadequately. The pages of Monteverdi's

"Orfeo" contain some of the grandest declamation ever conceived by a musician, and even on the concert stage, dissociated from its context and its essential operatic surroundings, it should make an extraordinary effect. But the modern singer does not know how to sing it. In fact he does not even try to sing it; he tries to declaim it in the modern way and that way is foreign to its style. This recitative demands a perfect legato, to which the modern declamatory style is radically hostile. It calls for long sweeping phrases, a deep breathed, organ like utterance, a grand and inspiring flow of noble tone.

This was the fundamental feature of the first operas. But the insatiable appetite of the hearer for sensuous amusement soon stripped the royal robes from this priestly art. And when the opera house was created and the public invited to the feast, the opera of the seventeenth century began its long and futile struggle to effect a compromise between its original artistic purpose and a desire to satisfy the public ear.

It was a sorry time in the history of Italian thought. The political condition of the country, with the heel of the Spanish oppressor on her throat, was pitiful, and her writers have left behind them a record of their utter failure to conceive ideas. Their works are costumes of conceits and whimsies and tawdry decorations draped upon thematic dummies. Independence of thought and action suppressed, learning discouraged, literature moribund, music became the chief pastime of a people without artistic convictions. It had no policy to promulgate, no opinions to publish, no theories to establish. It was but an empty toy, a specious imitation of the classic drama, and in a few short years it became a mere parade ground for arrogant and pampered performers, prestidigitators of scales and jugglers of trills.

In the early years of the opera, as we have said, the shadow of the red robe still hung over lyric art. The recitatives with concluding cadenzas and the psalms with final flourishes were constructed on the same plan. The custom of allotting all the chief roles in opera to high voices was only a part of the preservation of the ecclesiastic atmosphere. It was an unconscious movement in the direction of impersonality, always a primary requisite of the music of the sanctuary. One perceives a touch of innocent humor in the vivacious account given in a letter of Gobert to Huygens (1647) in reference to the Italians taken to Paris by the Cardinal Mazarin:

"There are four men and eight castrati, brought over by M. le Cardinal." The castrato might sing any kind of part. He could be called upon to impersonate a Roman emperor or a woman, Perseus or Achilles, Jupiter or Mercury. The absence of individuality in his sexless song entirely escaped the attention of a public trained to regard music as an aesthetic abstraction and the voice as a technical instrument.

Applying this consideration to our examination of the ideals of singing cherished in the sixteenth, seventeenth and most of the eighteenth century, we more readily perceive that sculpturesque beauty of style was the ultimate aim of the great artist, and that this end became obscured only when a voluptuary public, insatiable in its desire, clamored for more and more amazing feats of the virtuoso. In the early years of the seventeenth century the style of singing was distinguished by its limpid purity of tone, its perfect diction, its long drawn and exquisitely graded phrases, its elegant delivery of passages and ornaments. Speed was not a desideratum. The astonishment of the hearer by the emission of a great number of notes in a second began with the vocal gymnastics of the latter part of the century. In the first part the aim of the singer was to do everything elegantly and with finish, but not swiftly. His emotional range was limited to the grave, the contemplative and the pathetic.

In previous chapters we have reproduced comments on the art of some of the great exponents of seventeenth century singing. We may return to this art to glance at the achievements of the great Leonora Baroni, characteristic of her time. Some of her contemporaries charged her with being her own "press agent," as we should express it to-day; but it is difficult to believe that in a period in which the art of advertising was so crude she could thus have chained popes and world famous poets to her triumphal chariot wheels.

Leonora's mother, Adriana, was also a famous singer and the teacher of her daughter. The latter was born in 1611. Interesting facts about her are assembled in Romain Rolland's delightful "Musiciens d'Autrefois." It was in February, 1644, that Mazarin despatched an order to the French ambassador at Rome to send Leonora to Paris and to give her a thousand pistoles for the journey and as much for a yearly allowance. Mazarin had dwelt long in the Barberini Palace in Rome and there had heard operas of the new school and also this apparently incomparable singer. Maugars, who wrote a work with a cumbersome title, * says that she was "the wonder of the world who made me forget my mortal state, so that I thought I was really among the angels, sharing the joys of the blessed."

One easily suspects that this divine Leonora had something more than voice and art to enchain the souls of the male sex, for Pope Clement IX called her a "sweet siren" and made particular mention of her glowing eyes. Forty Italian poets made a book of verses in her honor: "Applausi Poetici alle Glorie della Signora Baroni." But this was not all. John Milton attended an operatic performance at the Barberini palace in 1639 and straightway indited a Latin sonnet "Ad Leonoram Romae Canentem."

"Altera Torquatum cepit Leonora poetam cujus ab insano
    cessit amore furens.
Ah! miser ille tuo quanto felicius aevo perditus, et propter
    te, Leonora, foret!"

These literary adorations, however, signified less than the more active proceedings of the Cardinal with his thousands of pistoles. He had Leonora carried to Paris, where he lodged her in the house adjoining his own and caused her

* Réponse fait a un curieux sur le sentiment de la musique de l'Italie, escrite a Rome le premier Octobre, 1639.

to be attended by his own servants. Maugars constituted himself defender of the fair fame of the singer and endeavored to strengthen his position by denying to her that beauty which enraptured a pope. In the passage in which he does this he also tells us of her art.

"She has excellent judgment and knows good music from bad. She can listen intelligently and even composes herself. In her singing she perfectly expresses the meaning of the words. She does not pride herself on being beautiful, but she is neither distasteful to the eye nor coquettish. She sings without restraint, with true modesty and with a sweet seriousness. Her voice is of a high compass, true, sonorous and melodious, and she softens or increases the tone without any trouble and without making grimaces. Her transports and her sighs are never voluptuous, her glances are never indecorous, and her gestures have the seemliness of a virtuous girl. In passing from one note to another she sometimes makes one feel intervals of an enharmonic and chromatic kind with skill and charm."

We need not concern ourselves with the mystic meaning of the last sentence, but may be content noting that at the time of her adventure into Paris the bewitching Leonora was 33 years old and possessed a husband, one Giulio Cesare Castellani, of whom singularly little is recorded. Signora Baroni was not an opera singer, but, like her famous elder contemporary, Vittoria Archilei, a virtuosa di musica da camera, a chamber singer. Some of the French courtiers did not greatly admire her art at first, but her majesty the Queen put the seal of her approbation on it and silenced all opposition. The prima donna was accorded access to the queen's apartments at all hours and the royal hand bestowed upon her "ten thousand francs to dress herself in the French style, a collar of pearls, earrings and a warrant for several thousand crowns' worth of jewels and a warrant for an allowance of a thousand crowns."

What a pity it is that we have not similar accounts of the Parisian experiences of Anna Manarini, a soprano of the middle of the seventeenth century, who went with Cavalli to the French capital to "create" leading roles in his popular operas. But since we have made such a point of the elegance and finish of the singing of these years and insisted that power was not a desideratum, let us note that when exceptionally big voices were found, they were not left idle. Filanti, a tenor robusto of the second half of the seventeenth century, was noted for the tremendous volume of his voice and accordingly composers wrote airs for him in which he could display it. The production of airs of a florid type with trumpet obbligato was not unknown, but those written for Filanti featured power. In an air of this kind in Legrenzi's "Scylla" Filanti, as our newspapers would say, "created a sensation." The same style of composition was not unknown in England and Henry Purcell (1658-1695) wrote several such airs. One notes in passing the success of Mr. Bowen in the great aria with two trumpets in "The Libertine Destroyed"—the hero being no less a personage than Don Giovanni. We find also that the performer of vocal feats could not always obscure the histrionic genius. Marthe Lerochois, a singer at the Grand Opera of Paris from 1678 to 1697, shone by her talent as a tragedian and by the grandeur of her declamation rather than her vocal virtuosity. Her contemporaries praised the splendor of her eyes, the nobility of her gesture and the dramatic puissance of her delivery.

All these early artists labored vigorously to reach their ends. They knew no short cuts to fame and fortune, these singers of the golden age. There seem to have been no teachers who advertised to secure engagements at the Venetian opera houses after one year's study. Mazzochi lifts the veil of seclusion from a seventeenth century Roman school in which church singers were trained:

"The pupils were obliged to devote every day one hour to the practice of difficult pieces in order to acquire the necessary experience. Three hours were distributed, one to trills, the second to passages, and the third to ornaments. During another hour the pupil worked, under the master's direction, placed before a mirror, in order that he might acquire no contortions of the eyes, the face or mouth in singing.

"Such were the occupations of the morning. In the afternoon theory was studied for half an hour, an hour was devoted to the study of counterpoint and another to the study of letters. For the rest of the day the student exercised on the clavecin or in the composition of a psalm, motet or other kind of piece according to his talent."

It is in the labors and the ideals of the singers and teachers of the sixteenth and seventeenth centuries that we find everything fashioned and defined that became the glory of the famous eighteenth century virtuosi. We cannot discover in the summaries of the teachings of the schools of the eighteenth century, as preserved in the writings of Tosi and Mancini, anything unknown to the masters of the period surveyed in this work. Tosi treated chiefly of the ornaments of florid song and the singer's musicianship. He tells us that a correct tone is neither nasal nor throaty and that it is to be taught by example. Perfect intonation is also demanded. The greatest care must be taken with the solmization of pupils to see that they sing in tune and that the voice "comes aforth neat and clear without passing through the nose or being choked in the throat." A series of graded studies was required. Chest, head and falsetto registers were noted and the union of them was demanded. A perfect portamento and a perfect messa di voce were needed. There were long exercises on shakes and divisions. Mancini covers the same ground except in recognizing only two registers instead of three. He gives specific directions for covering the break.

What have such masters to offer that is more valuable than the precepts handed down to us by Bovicelli, Caccini and Severi? It is quite certain that the whole body of vocal technic is well developed in the writings of these old masters and that the vocalises published in the seventeenth century contain the entire materials of the technic of song. Furthermore it is undeniable that the artistic ideals which supported the lyric art of the early years of the seventeenth century ought to endure as long as the art itself. To sing beautifully demands first and foremost a perfectly pure tone delivered in a sustained and smooth stream. This is the true river of song. Upon its surface the shimmer of sunlit wavelets of ornament or passage work shall float calmly and securely, diversifying its beauty, but not fundamentally altering it.

The singer who has mastered what the teachers of Bovicelli's age were teaching will find no difficulty in delivering the measures of Mozart. Nor will he, if he intelligently applies the fundamental law, find himself in trouble when he essays to publish the musical thought of Wagner or Verdi.

INDEX